DiRTY VEGAN

DIRTY VEGAN

FAST and EASY

Matt Pritchard

TOTALLY AWESOME VEGAN RECIPES

hamlyn

THIS BOOK IS DEDICATED TO MY LITTLE FAMILY, CIARA and OUR DOG LEMMY.
WHEN I DIDN'T LOVE MYSELF, OR WAS HARD TO LOVE, THE TWO OF THEM WERE
ALWAYS THERE TO PICK ME UP AND PUT A SMILE ON MY FACE. I LOVE YOU BOTH.

First published in Great Britain in 2023 by Hamlyn,
an imprint of Octopus Publishing Group Ltd
Carmelite House
50 Victoria Embankment
London EC4Y 0DZ
www.octopusbooks.co.uk

An Hachette UK Company
www.hachette.co.uk

ISBN 978-0-60063-785-1

A CIP catalogue record for this book is available from the British Library.

Printed and bound in China

13 5 7 9 10 8 6 4 2

Publishing Director Eleanor Maxfield
Editorial Director Natalie Bradley
Senior Editor Pauline Bache
Design and Art Direction Smith & Gilmour
Photographer Jamie Orlando Smith
Food Stylist and Recipe Development Phil Mundy
Props Stylist Hannah Wilkinson
Cover Illustrator Andy Smith
Art Director Jaz Bahra
Assistant Production Managers Nic Jones and Lucy Carter

CONTENTS

★ INTRODUCTION ★

I'm sitting here on my sofa thinking of what to say for this introduction. If I'm honest, I feel incredibly lucky that I'm even writing it. Back in 2018 when I got the green light to write a cookbook after filming *Dirty Vegan*, I could not believe it! Fast forward five years later, I'm sitting here writing my third, yep, my *third* book. Thank you for all your support on the last two books and TV series. And, if you're new to my cooking, welcome, and I hope you enjoy this one.

When I first started out with these books, my aim was always to provide simple plant-based recipes for everyone. As some are aware, it was at catering college when I first gained my cooking skills. I don't see myself as a first-class chef but as a good cook who enjoys creating dishes. I like simple homemade recipes and I believe that for most of us, when we come home after a hard day's work, the thought of opening a book and finding a recipe with an ingredients list the length of the M4 corridor and a method with as many words as the Bible is not appealing. So instead, if you like the sound of fast and easy cooking, well I wrote this book just for you! It's filled with simple but hearty recipes that are easy to follow and don't take up too much head space.

When it comes to the weekend, however, we ususally have a little time on our hands, and might fancy spending a bit more time in the kitchen. *Then* we can go rock a more complex recipe. So I've included a chapter for you to impress new dates and old mates as well. In addition, there are some ideas to stretch out basic ingredients across three meals, and invest the time in the kitchen when you have it – such as in my make-your-own-tofu recipe, which then has quick and easy ideas for how to use your deliciously home-crafted tofu. Of course, if you're *always* in a mega rush, shop-bought works too!

Being in the kitchen is extremely therapeutic for me; as someone who suffers with anxiety and self-confidence, I find it helps me focus. I was working to an incredibly tight deadline with this book and, to be honest, it couldn't have come at a better time. We have all experienced the last few years in different ways, but it's been a tough time for all. After the madness of the pandemic onset in 2020, I rowed the Atlantic Ocean from Lanzarote to Antigua in January 2021. After that was completed, I went from an extreme high to a major low and found myself slipping into old ways along with a lack of enthusiasm. As you all know I love a challenge and this book was exactly what I needed to get my cooking back on track in a simple, approachable manner.

Ladies and gents, boys and girls, freaks and uniques, I give to you my third cookbook. I really hope you all enjoy it as much as I enjoyed creating it for you.

Broccoli and peas,
Pritch
x

CHAPTER 1

BUNG IT ALL IN ONE POT

THAI-STYE GREEN CURRY 12

THAI-STYLE RED CURRY 14

SWEET POTATO AND 'CHICKEN' CURRY 15

MINESTRONE SOUP 16

ROASTED ROOT VEG FEAST AND
TURKISH ONION SALAD 19

RA-TA-TA-TOUILLE 21

VEGETABLE GOCHUJANG STEW 22

SMOKY DARK CHOCOLATE CHILLI 24

MOROCCAN-SPICED VEG AND LENTIL CASSEROLE 26

BREKKIE FRITTATA 28

SATAY SPUD, TOFU AND ASPARAGUS TRAY BAKE 29

CUPBOARD-LEFTOVER HOTPOT 30

This chapter title just about says it all: 'bung it all in a pot'. That can only mean one thing...very little washing up. Another bonus is it's great if you're just starting out cooking and don't have a lot of kit – you just need one pan, a chopping board, a knife and your ingredients, and you're good to go.

THAI-STYLE GREEN CURRY

SERVES 4

For the curry paste
1 tablespoon coriander seeds
1 tablespoon cumin seeds
6 rocket chillies or your
    choice of chilli
2 stalks of lemongrass
1 large shallot, peeled
2.5-cm (1-inch) piece of
    fresh root ginger, peeled
handful of coriander,
    including the stalks
handful of Thai basil, reserving
    a few sprigs to serve
peel of ½ lime
1 tablespoon vegan fish sauce
salt and pepper

For the curry
800ml (28fl oz) canned
    coconut milk
2 makrut lime leaves
150g (5½ oz) mushrooms,
    trimmed and quartered
1 green pepper, cored,
    deseeded and thickly sliced
2 carrots, peeled into long
    ribbons or thinly sliced
350g (12oz) head of broccoli,
    cut into small florets and
    the stem thinly sliced
handful of Thai basil (swap for
    Italian basil with a bit of mint
    if unavailable), torn
microwave rice or rice noodles,
    to serve (optional)

When making a Thai-inspired curry, it's always a good idea to make the paste from scratch – it brings so much flavour and aroma to the sauce. I also find the process to be very therapeutic. If you haven't got time to make the paste, you can buy some from your local supermarket and follow the rest of the recipe. And if you like this recipe, check out the Thai-style Red Curry on page 14.

Make the curry paste. Toast the coriander and cumin seeds in a small frying pan over medium heat for 1–2 minutes, shaking the pan to release the oils.

Using a pestle and mortar, smash the chillies into a pulp. Add the lemongrass and grind. Continue down the list of ingredients, until the aromas of the paste hit your nose. Add the ground coriander and cumin. Your paste is now ready to rock. (Leftover curry paste can be stored in the fridge for up to a week.)

Now, make the curry. Tip half of the coconut milk into a wok over medium-high heat and stir until thickened. Stir in half of the curry paste and cook for 3–4 minutes. Add the remaining coconut milk and lime leaves.

Chuck in the mushrooms and green pepper and cook for 2–3 minutes. Add the carrots and broccoli and cook for another 3–4 minutes.

Meanwhile, cook your rice or rice noodles, if using, according to packet instructions. Stir the Thai basil into the curry until it wilts. Discard the lime leaves.

Serve the curry in a bowl on its own or on top of the rice or rice noodles. Enjoy!

THAI-STYLE RED CURRY

SERVES 2

For the curry paste
4 Scotch bonnet chillies
8 garlic cloves
2 shallots, peeled
2 makrut lime leaves
2 stalks of lemongrass
2.5-cm (1-inch) piece of
    fresh root ginger, peeled
1 teaspoon palm sugar
1 teaspoon vegan fish sauce
1 teaspoon tamarind paste
salt and pepper

For the curry
virgin olive oil, for frying
1 red pepper, cored,
    deseeded and chopped
130g (4¾oz) baby sweetcorn
125g (4½oz) shiitake mushrooms
100g (3½oz) mangetout
10g (¼oz) edamame beans
2 tablespoons tomato purée
600ml (20fl oz) coconut milk
handful of Thai basil, chopped
    (see Note)
250g (9oz) silken tofu,
    cut into cubes
microwave rice, to serve

Thai curries come in a variety of colours with red being the hottest, yellow being the mildest and green falling somewhere in between. The Scotch bonnets add an intense heat, but if you're not into mind-numbing spice, just adjust it according to your preference.

Make the curry paste. Using a pestle and mortar, smash the chillies into a pulp. Add the next ingredient and grind. Continue down the list of ingredients, until you have a nice paste and that fragrant smell is hitting your nose.

Now make the curry. Heat 1 tablespoon of oil in a large frying pan over medium heat. Add the pepper, sweetcorn, mangetout and edamame and sauté for 5 minutes. Stir in the tomato purée and cook for another 3 minutes. Add a dessert spoon of the curry paste into the pan along with half of the coconut milk and stir. Cook for 5 minutes.

Pour in the remaining half of the coconut milk, then stir in the Thai basil. Bring to a simmer. Add the tofu, gently stirring to prevent the cubes from breaking up. Cook for 5 minutes. Meanwhile, cook your rice according to packet instructions.

Transfer the to a serving dish and serve with the rice.

SWEET POTATO and CHICKEN RED CURRY

SERVES 2

For the red curry paste
4 garlic cloves
3 red chillies, or to taste
3 makrut lime leaves
2 stalks of lemongrass
1 shallot, peeled
2.5-cm (1-inch) piece of fresh
    root ginger, peeled
30g (1oz) coriander, stems
    chopped and leaves reserved
1 teaspoon vegan fish sauce
1 teaspoon palm sugar

For the curry
3 sweet potatoes, cut into
    bite-sized pieces
virgin olive oil, for frying
1 onion, thinly sliced
1 red pepper, cored,
    deseeded and thinly sliced
500g (1lb 2oz) vegan chicken
400ml (14fl oz) coconut milk
microwave rice, to serve

NOTE
Leftover curry paste can be stored
in the fridge for up to 1 week.

Hands up, who loves a good curry? Well, I do. Back in the day, we'd hit the clubs until they closed in the wee hours of the morning. Afterwards, we'd head over to a curry house and my order of choice was the dopiaza curry, made with chicken, onions, ginger and garlic paste, chilli and a lot of spices. These days, I'm over late-night clubbing and chicken. So, instead, I prepare my own curry and it's every bit as good, if not better.

Make the curry paste. Combine all the ingredients, except the coriander leaves, in a blender and blend until smooth. (Alternatively, smash it all up in a pestle and mortar, which is far more satisfying after a hard day!)

Make the curry. Now's the time to cook your rice according to packet instructions.

Bring a saucepan of water to a boil. Add the sweet potatoes and boil for 7–10 minutes, until softened. Drain, then set aside.

Meanwhile, heat 1 tablespoon of oil in a frying pan over medium heat. Add the onion and pepper and sweat for 10 minutes. Add your vegan chicken and cook for the length of time indicated on the packet. Add half the curry paste, the coconut milk and sweet potatoes. Simmer for 10 minutes.

Meanwhile, cook your rice according to packet instructions. Finely chop the reserved coriander leaves. Reserve a little for the garnish, then stir the rest into the curry pan. Transfer the curry to a dish, garnish with the remaining coriander and serve with the rice.

MINESTRONE SOUP

SERVES 4

virgin olive oil, for frying
1 red onion, finely chopped
3 garlic cloves, finely chopped
7 leaves of green cabbage,
    finely chopped
3 tomatoes, finely chopped
2 carrots, finely chopped
2 celery sticks, finely chopped
1 parsnip, finely chopped
½ small swede, finely chopped
1 tablespoon tomato purée
400g (14oz) can adzuki beans,
    butter beans or your choice
    of beans, drained and rinsed
1 litre (1¾ pints) hot
    vegetable stock
400g (14oz) passata
squirt of tomato ketchup
2 bay leaves
1 bouquet garni of sage and
    oregano, tied into a bunch
    with kitchen string
100g (3½oz) spaghetti,
    broken into short lengths
salt and pepper

To serve
sliced crusty baguette
extra virgin olive oil

I've loved minestrone soup since I was a kid, and this fortifying winter warmer is full of goodness. The store-bought variety pales in comparison, so take the time to prepare the soup from scratch – it'll be well worth your efforts.

Make the soup. Heat 1 tablespoon of oil in a large saucepan over medium heat. Add the onion and sweat for 7 minutes, until translucent. Add the garlic and sauté for another 2 minutes. Add the cabbage, tomatoes, carrots, celery, parsnip and swede and stir. Cover and sweat 7 minutes.

Stir in the tomato purée and cook for 1 minute. Add the beans, then pour in the vegetable stock, passata and ketchup. Give it a mix. Add the bay leaves and bouquet garni. Season with salt and pepper. Bring to a boil, then reduce the heat to medium-low and simmer for 5 minutes.

Add the broken spaghetti, cover and cook for 12–15 minutes, until the pasta and veg are cooked. Season to taste with salt and pepper.

Ladle soup into bowls and serve hot with crusty baguette slices with a drizzle of extra virgin olive oil.

GUEST CHEF: TUBBY TOM
ROASTED ROOT VEG FEAST and TURKISH ONION SALAD
SERVES 2-4

6 tablespoons rapeseed oil,
   preferably smoked
1 red onion, thinly sliced
handful of flat-leaf parsley,
   chopped, plus extra
   to garnish
pinch of sumac
pinch of sugar
pinch of sea salt
125ml (4fl oz) lime juice
2 garlic bulbs
4 carrots, cut into thick batons
4 parsnips, cut into thick batons
2 sweet potatoes, cut into
   thick batons
1 swede, cut into thick batons
60g (2¼oz) kebab seasoning
   (I used Pritchard × Tubby
   special edition Roots Radical
   Shawarma Super Kebab Rub)
300g (10½oz) vegan
   Greek yogurt
2 tablespoons mint sauce

I once met someone at an event who suggested I check out Tubby Tom's sauces. I searched them out on Instagram and immediately fell in love with the branding so I had to pay them a visit. Their warehouse was unbelievable – it was stocked full of chilli sauces, herby rubs and other sauces as far as the eye could see. I brought home a selection and I've been using them ever since. We released a collab chilli sauce a while back and now we have this incredible Roots Radical rub. Tubby's recipe here is banging. Don't worry about cutting the veggie batons neatly. Why? Scraggily bits = crispy edges.

Preheat the oven to 200°C (400°F), Gas Mark 6. Add 4 tablespoons of oil to a roasting pan and pop it into the oven to warm up.

In a bowl, combine the onion, parsley, sumac, sugar, salt and lime juice. Toss to mix and set aside.

Slice a few millimetres off the top of the garlic bulbs so you can just see a little flesh of the garlic cloves inside their papery skins. Drizzle a tablespoon of oil over both the bulbs.

Carefully remove the pan from the oven. Gently slide the garlic and veggies into the pan to minimize any splashing of hot oil. Toss to coat.

Roast for 30 minutes, shaking the pan every 10 minutes. Remove the pan from the oven. Add the seasoning, shake it again, then roast for another 20 minutes, until crispy and golden brown. Keep an eye on it – you don't want it to burn. If it appears to be getting to brown, reduce the heat.

Meanwhile, make your yoggy sauce. Mix the yogurt and mint sauce in a small bowl. Done!

Remove the roasting pan from the oven. Stir in the onion salad. Drizzle with the yoggy sauce. Garnish with parsley and give yourself a pat on the back.

RA-TA-TA-TOUILLE

SERVES 2

virgin olive oil, for frying
1 red onion, finely chopped
2 aubergines, finely chopped
2 courgettes, finely chopped
1 red, yellow or green pepper,
    cored, deseeded and
    finely chopped
5 tomatoes, chopped
400g (14oz) can plum tomatoes
1 teaspoon tomato purée
4 garlic cloves, finely chopped
2 sprigs of thyme
15g (½oz) basil, chopped
salt and pepper
steamed rice, mashed potatoes,
    couscous or quinoa,
    to serve (optional)

My mother often prepared ratatouille for when we were young; she'd rustle up a batch whenever she was short of ingredients. I eat this on its own hot or cold, but you can also serve it with rice, mashed potatoes, couscous or quinoa.

Heat 1 tablespoon of oil in a casserole over medium heat. Add the onion and sweat for 7 minutes, until softened and translucent. Put the onion in a bowl.

Add another tablespoon of oil to the casserole. Add the aubergines and cook for 5 minutes, until softened. Transfer the aubergines to the same bowl. Repeat with the courgettes and the pepper, adding a little more oil if necessary.

Add the fresh and canned tomatoes, crushing the plum tomatoes in your hands first. Stir in the tomato purée, then add the garlic. Cook for 3 minutes, then add all of the cooked vegetables.

Chuck in the thyme and basil and stir to mix. Season with salt and pepper.

Serve with rice, potatoes, couscous or quinoa, if you wish.

VEGETABLE GOCHUJANG STEW

SERVES 4

virgin olive oil, for frying
1 leek, trimmed, cleaned
    and sliced
2 celery sticks, chopped
150g (5½oz) mushrooms,
    trimmed and halved
5 garlic cloves, finely chopped
2 tablespoons gochujang paste
1 teaspoon red or white
    miso paste
900ml (32fl oz) vegetable stock
1 carrot, roughly chopped
300g (10½oz) baby
    potatoes, halved
2 sweetcorn, cobs
    cut into quarters
1 large courgette,
    roughly chopped
1 tablespoon cornflour
1 tablespoon water
handful flat-leaf parsley
    or coriander, plus
    extra to garnish
salt and pepper

If chilli heat isn't your thing, this ain't the dish for you. Thanks to the gochujang, this hearty stew has a proper kick. Gochujang is a spicy Korean paste made with red chilli peppers, fermented soy beans, rice and salt. I remember how difficult it was to find a number of years ago, so I would buy it online. These days, it's available in most supermarkets.

Heat 2 tablespoons of oil in a casserole over medium-high heat. Add the leek, celery and mushrooms and sweat for 5 minutes. Add the garlic and cook for another minute.

Stir in the gochujang and miso and cook for another minute. Pour in the vegetable stock. Add the carrot and potatoes, season with salt and pepper and bring to a boil. Reduce the heat to medium-low and simmer for 20 minutes. Add the corn and courgette.

In a small bowl, combine the cornflour and measured water. Stir it into the pan to thicken the sauce.

Stir in the parsley or coriander and season to taste with salt and pepper.

Transfer the stew to a serving bowl or serve it out of the casserole, with the extra parsley or coriander to garnish. FYI: The sweetcorn should be cool enough to pick up with your hands to eat. That's right, it's time to get your fingers dirty.

SMOKY DARK CHOCOLATE CHILLI

SERVES 4

2 tablespoons sunflower oil

1 onion, diced

1 red pepper, cored, deseeded and finely chopped

5 garlic cloves, finely chopped

2 teaspoons mild chilli powder, or to taste

1 teaspoon ground cumin

1 teaspoon ground coriander

2 tablespoons tomato purée

2 teaspoons chipotle paste

500g (1lb 2oz) plant mince

400g (14oz) can kidney beans, drained and rinsed

400g (14oz) can chopped tomatoes

400g (14oz) passata

1 tablespoon liquid smoke or 1 teaspoon smoked paprika

1 tablespoon tomato ketchup

100g (3½oz) dark vegan chocolate (70% cocoa), roughly chopped

200ml (7fl oz) vegetable stock

salt and pepper

flat-leaf parsley, roughly torn, to garnish

To serve

Vegan Crème Fraîche (see page 129)

rice or baked potato (optional)

Chilli has been my favourite dish ever since my mother first cooked it for us when I was a child. When I'd come home from school and ask what was for dinner, it always put a smile on my face when Mam shouted 'Chilli'! In fact, she taught me how to make it. My first book featured my Four/Five/Six-Bean Chilli, but this smoky version is made with plant mince and rich dark chocolate. It goes so well with rice, baked spuds or even just a bowl of it on its lonesome.

Heat the oil in a casserole over medium heat. Add the onion and pepper and sweat for 7 minutes, until softened. Add the garlic and cook for another 2–3 minutes.

Add the chilli powder, cumin and coriander. Stir in the tomato purée and chipotle paste and cook for 2–3 minutes.

Add the plant mince and cook for 5 minutes, or as indicated on the packet instructions. Stir in the kidney beans, canned tomatoes and passata. Season with salt and pepper.

Add the liquid smoke (or smoked paprika), ketchup and dark vegan chocolate. Pour in the vegetable stock and mix well. Reduce the heat to low and simmer for 30 minutes, stirring occasionally. If the mixture seems too dry, add a splash of water.

Season to taste with more salt and pepper. Garnish with the parsley.

Serve the chilli on its own with vegan crème fraiche, over steamed rice or on top of a baked spud.

MOROCCAN-SPICED VEG and LENTIL CASSEROLE

SERVES 4

For the spice blend
1 teaspoon smoked paprika
1 teaspoon ground allspice
1 teaspoon ground coriander
1 teaspoon ground cinnamon
1 teaspoon ground cumin
1 teaspoon ground turmeric

For the casserole
virgin olive oil, for frying
1 onion, finely chopped
5 garlic cloves, finely chopped
2 carrots, cut into 2.5-cm
    (1-inch) chunks
2 parsnips, cut into 2.5-cm
    (1-inch) chunks
1 turnip, cut into 2.5-cm
    (1-inch) chunks
400g (14oz) can
    chopped tomatoes
200g (7oz) can green
    lentils, rinsed
100g (3½oz) raisins
500ml (18fl oz) vegetable stock
½ cauliflower, separated into
    florets (see Note)
2 teaspoons harissa paste
500ml (18fl oz) water
100g (3½oz) giant couscous
handful of flat-leaf parsley
salt and pepper

NOTE
Discarded cauliflower leaves
can be kept in the fridge and
cooked like cabbage.

*I've always been fascinated by Morocco and its bazaars:
the spices, the colours, the hustle and bustle... it's definitely
on my bucket list. Their most popular culinary exports
are probably tagine and couscous, both of which I love.
Here, I've made a hearty veggie stew with giant couscous
(also known as pearl couscous or mograbieh).*

Make the spice blend. Combine all the ingredients in
a small bowl. Set aside.

Make the casserole. Heat 2 tablespoons of oil in a casserole
over medium heat. Add the onion and garlic and sweat for
5 minutes, until softened. Add the spice blend and cook
for 3 minutes. Do not let the spices burn.

Add the carrots, parsnips and turnip and sauté them
for 5 minutes.

Add the canned tomatoes, lentils and raisins. Pour in
the vegetable stock. Cover, then reduce the heat to low
and gently simmer for 35 minutes, until the vegetables
are nearly cooked. Add the cauliflower florets and stir
in the harissa paste. Cook for another 10 minutes.

Meanwhile, bring the measured water to a boil in a small
saucepan. Add the giant couscous, cover and cook for
8–10 minutes.

Add the parsley to the casserole. Season with salt
and pepper.

It's now ready. Serve the stew with warm couscous.

BREKKIE FRITTATA

SERVES 4

For the 'egg' mixture
450g (1lb) firm tofu
300g (10½oz) silken tofu
100g (3½oz) shredded
    vegan cheese
4 tablespoon nutritional yeast
½ teaspoon black salt (see Note)
½ teaspoon ground white pepper
½ teaspoon ground turmeric
125ml (4fl oz) plant-based milk
1 teaspoon Dijon mustard
salt and pepper

For the frittata
1 tablespoon sunflower oil
300g (10½oz) vegan sausages,
    cut into chunks
1 red pepper, cored,
    deseeded and chopped
1 green pepper, cored,
    deseeded and chopped
150g (5½oz) button
    mushrooms, halved
3 spring onions, thinly sliced
2 garlic cloves, crushed
handful of parsley, chopped
1 red or green chilli, chopped,
    or chilli flakes (optional)
600g (1lb 5oz) hash browns,
    enough to cover the pan
100g (3½oz) shredded
    vegan cheese
200g (7oz) baby
    tomatoes, halved

NOTE
Black salt is a kiln-fired rock
salt with a distinct sulphurous
scent. Sub it with regular salt
if it's unavailable.

Want a full brekkie but you find yourself constantly messing up all the timings? You know, when the vegan sausages are ready but the hash browns are still in the oven? Or vice versa. Then, you have to reheat something in the microwave so each item is equally hot on the plate. Urgh. Fear not, gang. This all-in-one brekkie break is an absolute treat and super easy to put together – it's perfect for the morning after the night before!

Preheat the oven to 180°C (350°F), Gas Mark 4.

Make the 'egg' mixture. Combine all the ingredients in a blender and whizz until smooth. Season to taste with salt and pepper. Transfer the mixture to a bowl, then set aside.

Make the frittata. Heat the oil in a medium (approximately 24cm/9½ inch), ovenproof frying pan over medium-high heat. Add the sausages and cook for 2–3 minutes, until they start to colour. Add the peppers and mushrooms and cook for another 5 minutes. Stir in the spring onions, garlic, parsley and chilli, if using. Cook for 30 seconds, then remove from the heat. Add the contents to the 'egg' mixture. Stir in half the tomatoes.

Arrange the hash browns in a single layer in the base of the frying pan. Tip the 'egg' mixture into the pan and spread out evenly. Sprinkle with the vegan cheese and tomatoes. Bake for 45 minutes, until the middle is just set and golden. Set aside for 10 minutes.

Serve it up! When I'm lucky enough to have any leftovers, I simply pop it in the fridge and enjoy it for breakfast the next day.

SATAY SPUD, TOFU and ASPARAGUS TRAY BAKE

· SERVES 4 ·

For the marinated tofu
½ garlic clove, crushed
1-cm (½-inch) piece of fresh
    root ginger, crushed
2 tablespoons soy sauce
1 tablespoon maple syrup
1 tablespoon lime juice
1 teaspoon toasted sesame oil
1 teaspoon ketchup
½ teaspoon hot sauce
½ teaspoon mild curry powder
450g (1lb) firm tofu, cut into
    bite-sized chunks

For the tray bake
virgin olive oil, for greasing
200g (7oz) waxy potatoes
    (Jersey Royals, Charlottes
    or fingerlings), halved
100g (3½oz) thick asparagus,
    trimmed (see Note)
2 red onions, keep core intact
    and quarter into wedges

For the satay sauce
3 tablespoons smooth or
    crunchy peanut butter
1 tablespoon soy sauce
1 tablespoon brown sugar
½ tablespoon cider vinegar
pinch of salt
200ml (7fl oz) coconut milk
1 tablespoon lime juice
2-cm (¾-inch) piece of fresh
    root ginger, finely chopped
1 garlic clove, finely chopped
crushed peanuts, to garnish
    (optional)

*Creamy peanut satay, seasoned tofu and spuds work a treat.
Add asparagus into the picture and you have yourself a winner
of a dinner. You may be reminded of this dish when you go
for a wee later on too, though not everyone can notice it.
Funny, hey?*

Make the marinade. In a small bowl, combine all the
ingredients, except for the tofu, and mix well. Add the tofu,
then mix to coat. Cover the bowl with clingfilm and refrigerate
for at least 1 hour but preferably overnight.

Prepare the tray bake. Preheat the oven to 220°C (425°F),
Gas Mark 7. Drizzle a roasting pan with oil.

Add the drained tofu, potatoes and onions to the prepared
pan. Drizzle with oil, season with salt and pepper and roast
for 30 minutes. Add the asparagus and another drizzle of oil
and roast for another 10 minutes, until the veg are tender.

Meanwhile, make your satay sauce. Combine all the
ingredients in a small saucepan and mix well. Heat over
medium heat until warmed through.

Remove the pan from the oven, drizzle with satay sauce and
garnish with crushed peanuts, if you wish.

NOTE
The easiest way to trim an asparagus is to bend it in half until it breaks.
It snaps at the perfect point.

CUPBOARD-LEFTOVER HOTPOT

SERVES 4

4 tablespoons Vegan Butter
(see page 36)
2 onions, thinly sliced
2 celery sticks, finely chopped
1 carrot, finely chopped
2 garlic cloves, finely chopped
3 tablespoons tomato purée
400g (14oz) plant mince
700ml (1¼ pints) vegetable
stock
150ml (5fl oz) red or white wine
1 tablespoon mushroom ketchup
or vegan Worcestershire sauce
1 teaspoon balsamic glaze
3 sprigs of thyme, leaves only
2 sprigs of sage, finely chopped
1 tablespoon cornflour
1 tablespoon water
400g (14oz) small potatoes,
scrubbed well and sliced
salt and pepper

My original plan was to prepare a vegan 'beef' and onion pie, but I had ingredients in my fridge that would make a better and more interesting option. As I despise wasting food, I always try to put leftovers to good use and prepare something creative. This recipe does just that: it's quick to prepare and full of flavour. Make sure to finely chop all your vegetables to ensure even cooking.

Preheat the oven to 190°C (375°F), Gas Mark 5.

Melt 2 tablespoons of vegan butter in a large casserole over medium heat. Add the onions, celery and carrot and sweat for 10 minutes, until softened. Add the garlic and tomato purée and cook for another 2 minutes.

Stir in the plant mince, vegetable stock, wine, mushroom ketchup or vegan Worcestershire sauce and balsamic glaze. Add the thyme and sage.

In a small bowl, mix the cornflour and measured water. Add to the mixture and simmer for 5 minutes, until thickened.

Layer the potatoes over the filling. Brush with the remaining 2 tablespoons of vegan butter. Cover loosely with foil or a lid and bake for 20 minutes. Uncover, then bake for another 15 minutes, until the liquid has reduced and the potatoes are tender.

Serve and dig in!

CHAPTER

2

CWTCH
FOOD

MAKE YOUR OWN WHITE BREAD AND VEGAN BUTTER 36

THREE WAYS WITH BREAD
LENTIL HUMMUS, ASPARAGUS AND POMEGRANATE ON TOAST 38
VEGAN 'TUNA' SANDWICH 39
CREAMED LEEKS AND PEAS ON TOAST 41

BAKED MAC AND SHEEZE 42

COCONUT CURRY AND CAULIFLOWER RICE 44

MOOOOOO-LESS 'BEEF' AND MUSHROOM PIE 46

BBQ PULLED MUSHROOM SANDWICH 48

CHEESY POTATO BALLS 50

THE ULTIMATE HANGOVER DIRTY FRIES 52

CREAMY ROAST GARLIC AND TOMATO PASTA 54

'TOFISH' AND CHIPPIES 56

GNOCCHI WITH BASIL AND SAGE PESTO 57

FLY-AWAY CAULIFLOWER BUFFALO BITES 58

BAKED SWEET POTATO WITH BEAN AND CHILLI SLAW 60

NACHOS 61

For all the Welsh people out there, you'll understand the word 'cwtch' and for all those that don't, well, it's pronounced like 'cutch' and it means a 'hug' or 'to give a hug'.

The recipes in this chapter are made to give you a nice, big, comforting cwtch.

MAKE YOUR OWN WHITE BREAD *and* VEGAN BUTTER

MAKES 1 LOAF
+ ABOUT 300G/
10OZ OF BUTTER

For the vegan butter
220g (7¾oz) coconut oil,
   at room temperature
175ml (6fl oz) plant-based milk
   (I used unsweetened soy milk)
3 tablespoons avocado oil
1 tablespoon nutritional yeast
1 teaspoon lemon juice
½ teaspoon flaky sea salt

For the bread
500g (1lb 2oz) strong
   white bread flour,
   plus extra for dusting
7g (¼oz) fast-action
   dried yeast
2 teaspoons salt
1 tablespoon olive oil,
   plus extra for greasing
300ml (10fl oz) water

Many years ago, my brother once said, 'Bread's the best invention ever – you can put anything between two slices.' He was right. Here's an easy recipe for a wholesome loaf of white bread. Sure, wholemeal is healthier, but white is okay in moderation. I've also prepared it with a homemade vegan butter (or plant butter – call it what you will). It is delicious with this bread, but it can be spread on toast or used for cooking. You can even level up on flavour by adding garlic or herbs.

Make the vegan butter. Line a dish with baking paper or muslin. Combine all the ingredients in a blender and blitz, until smooth. Pour into the prepared dish and freeze for 1 hour to set. This will then keep chilled in the fridge for up to a week.

Make the bread. Sift the flour into a big bowl. Stir in the yeast and salt. Make a little well in the centre, then pour in the oil and measured water and mix.

Now, it's time roll up your sleeves and get to work. Place the dough onto a lightly floured work surface and knead it for 10 minutes, until you feel a bead of sweat trickle down your forehead.

Lightly grease a clean, dry bowl with olive oil. Put the dough into the bowl and cover with clingfilm or a tea towel, then set aside in a warm room for about 2 hours, or until doubled in size.

Punch the air out of the dough, then shape it into a ball. Place it on a baking sheet lined with baking paper. Set aside to rest for 1 hour, until it's doubled in size again.

Once rested, preheat the oven to 200°C (400°F), Gas Mark 6. Make a decorative design of incisions on the top of the bread, taking care not to cut too deep. Bake for 30 minutes.

Knock on the bottom of the loaf in the same way you might knock a door. It should sound hollow. If not, pop it back in the oven for a few minutes. Set aside to cool.

Cut into thick slices and serve with vegan butter.

★ ✦★ ✦ THREE WAYS WITH BREAD ✦★ ✦ ★

★

*Jazz up your homemade loaf with these twists
on classic recipes.*

PREP 10 MINUTES ★ COOK 5 MINUTES

LENTIL HUMMUS, ASPARAGUS and POMEGRANATE ON TOAST

SERVES 2

For the hummus
400g (14oz) can
    brown lentils,
    drained and rinsed
2 garlic cloves
1 teaspoon ground cumin
1 tablespoon tahini
1 tablespoon lemon juice
1 tablespoon olive oil
salt and pepper

For the assembly
virgin olive oil, for drizzling
250g (9oz) asparagus,
    trimmed (see Note)
2 thick slices of Easy
    Peasy White Bread
    (see pages 36–7)
Vegan Butter (see page 36)
½ pomegranate

NOTE
The easiest way to trim an
asparagus is to bend it in
half until it breaks. It snaps
at the perfect point.

This is my take on hummus (which means 'chickpea' in Arabic).
Spread it generously on toast, then top with grilled asparagus
and tart pomegranate – it's incredible. Lentils are also a great
source of protein and fibre. I've prepared it with the Easy Peasy
White Bread (see pages 36–7), but you could replace it with a
store-bought bread.

Make the hummus. In a food processor, combine all the
ingredients and blitz until smooth or to your desired consistency.
If it seems a bit thick, add a splash of water. Season to taste
with salt and pepper.

Heat 1 tablespoon of oil on a griddle over medium heat. Add
the asparagus and cook for 3–5 minutes, until charred. Set aside.

Meanwhile, toast the bread, then generously spread with
vegan butter. Place the toast on a large plate, then spread on
the hummus. Sprinkle with pomegranate seeds and top with
grilled asparagus to serve, then pick it up with your hands
and scoff it down or be posh by using a knife and fork.

VEGAN 'TUNA' SANDWICH

SERVES 2

400g (14oz) can chickpeas, drained and rinsed (reserve the liquid to use as aquafaba in other recipes)
½ celery stick, finely chopped
¼ red onion, finely chopped
1 teaspoon capers or gherkins
80g (2¾oz) sweetcorn
1 tablespoon nori powder
100ml (3½fl oz) vegan mayonnaise
2 tablespoons lemon juice
1 teaspoon Dijon mustard
4 slices of Easy Peasy White Bread (see pages 36–7)
chopped iceberg lettuce (optional)
salt and pepper

I've spent most of my life on the road, travelling to skate comps, for demos and tours. Then came Dirty Sanchez, *and I was back on the road filming and touring our live show. This also means that I've spent a lot of time in service stations up and down the UK. Each one had a 'meal deal' offer, which included a pack of sandwiches, crisps and a drink. My go-to was the tuna and sweetcorn sandwich. Since turning vegan, I now make a version with chickpeas, sweetcorn and vegan mayo. It's delicious, filling and a thing of beauty.*

In a bowl, combine the chickpeas, celery, onion and capers. Using a potato masher, mash everything up until it almost resembles a rustic paste.

Add the sweetcorn, nori, mayo, lemon juice and Dijon. Mix well. Season to taste with salt and pepper.

Spread the mixture onto slices of bread. If you wish, add some iceberg lettuce for crunch.

Slice in half and serve.

CREAMED LEEKS and PEAS ON TOAST

SERVES 2

50g (1¾oz) Vegan Butter (see page 36)
1 large leek, trimmed, cleaned and halved lengthways
2 garlic cloves, crushed
100g (3½oz) frozen peas
3 sprigs of thyme
75ml (2½fl oz) plant-based cream
2 thick slices of Easy Peasy White Bread (see pages 36–7)
salt and pepper

A Welsh man cooking leeks sounds like a start of a joke, but it isn't. It really is a Welsh man cooking creamed leeks and peas on toast. This is awesome for brekkie or lunch.

Melt a good tablespoon of vegan butter in a frying pan over medium-high heat. Slice the leeks, then add to the pan. Sweat for 2 minutes, then add the garlic. Add the peas and thyme, then stir in the plant-based cream. Mix well, then season with salt and pepper. Simmer for 3 minutes.

Meanwhile, toast the bread. Place them on plates, then spread a generous amount of vegan butter on each slice. Top with creamed leeks and peas.

And bon voyage – you're on your way to comfort heaven.

BAKED MAC and SHEEZE

SERVES 4

250g (9oz) macaroni
virgin olive oil, for frying
120g (4¼oz) vegan bacon
100g (3½oz) Vegan Butter
 (see page 36)
100g (3½oz) plain flour
800ml (28fl oz) plant-based
 milk (I used oat)
200g (7oz) shredded
 vegan cheese, plus extra
 for sprinkling (I used
 Applewood Vegan Smoky
 Cheese Alternative)
4 tablespoons nutritional yeast
200g (7oz) peas
chilli flakes, for sprinkling
salt and white or black pepper

My memory of macaroni cheese as a kid was the tinned version from a very well-known brand, but this version is a LOT better for you and packed with flavour. The salty plant lardons work really well with the sheeze to give you a nice comforting cwtch with every mouthful.

Preheat the oven to 180°C (350°F), Gas Mark 4.

Cook the macaroni according to packet instructions.

Meanwhile, heat 1 tablespoon of olive oil in a frying pan over medium-high heat. Add the vegan bacon and cook for 3–5 minutes, until cooked through. Transfer to a chopping board and finely chop.

To make a roux, melt the vegan butter in a small saucepan over medium heat. Add the flour and mix until a paste forms. Gradually pour in the plant-based milk and mix until smooth. (It's important to add the milk slowly; otherwise, your sauce will separate and turn lumpy. And that's the last thing you want.)

Stir in the vegan cheese and mix until smooth. The sauce will look lumpy at first, but don't worry – it'll melt away and transform into a cheesy sauce. Stir in the nutritional yeast. Season to taste with salt and pepper.

Add the cooked macaroni to the sauce. Stir in the peas and vegan bacon. Transfer to an ovenproof dish, then sprinkle grated cheese on top. Bake for 20–25 minutes.

Sprinkle with chilli flakes. Dig in.

GUEST CHEF: THE DALY DISH
COCONUT CURRY and CAULIFLOWER RICE

SERVES 2

olive or rapeseed oil, for frying
1 onion, finely chopped
4 garlic cloves, minced
1 green chilli, finely
    sliced, or to taste
8–10 mushrooms,
    trimmed and quartered
2 carrots, sliced or grated
1 red pepper, cored, deseeded
    and roughly chopped
1 yellow pepper, cored, deseeded
    and roughly chopped
½ head of broccoli, chopped
400ml (14fl oz) coconut milk
2 tablespoons curry powder
1 teaspoon ground turmeric
200ml (7fl oz) vegetable stock
2 teaspoons cornflour
½ cauliflower, grated (see Note)
2 teaspoons water
salt and pepper

To garnish
2–3 spring onions, finely sliced
pinch of nigella seeds

NOTE
Discarded cauliflower leaves
can be kept in the fridge and
cooked like cabbage.

I met Gina and Karol at a gig in Dublin, touring the story of Dirty Sanchez, quite a few years ago. I was following their delicious recipes on Instagram so it was great to meet them in person. So thank you to Gina and Karol for this fantastic recipe of coconut curry and cauliflower rice. Hope you enjoy cooking this as much as I did.

Heat a tablespoon of oil in a deep pan or wok over medium-high heat. Add the onion, garlic and chilli and sweat for 5–7 minutes, until the onion is translucent. Add the mushrooms, carrots, peppers and broccoli and stir for 4–6 minutes.

Add the coconut milk, curry powder and turmeric. Stir well. Pour in the stock and stir. Bring to a boil, then reduce the heat and simmer for 10 minutes, until it begins to thicken.

In a small bowl, combine the cornflour with the measured water. Stir the mixture into the sauce and cook until thickened. Season to taste with salt and pepper. Keep warm.

Heat 1 tablespoon of oil in a frying pan over medium-high heat. Press the cauliflower in kitchen paper to remove excess moisture. Add the cauliflower to the pan and sauté for 5–6 minutes. (Or microwave on high for 3 minutes in a microwave-safe dish.)

Place the cauliflower rice on a serving platter, top with the curry and garnish with spring onions and nigella seeds.

MOOOOOO-LESS 'BEEF' and MUSHROOM PIE

· SERVES 2 ·

20g (¾oz) dried
    porcini mushrooms
175ml (6fl oz)
    boiling water
2 tablespoons
    sunflower oil
280g (10oz) plant mince
    or steaks, chopped
2 onions, roughly
    chopped
5 garlic cloves,
    finely chopped
350g (12oz) chestnut
    mushrooms, trimmed
    and halved
4 tablespoons plain flour
400ml (14fl oz) dry stout
    (I used Guinness)
150ml (5fl oz) strong
    vegetable stock
7 sprigs of thyme
2 teaspoons maple syrup
320g (11¼oz) vegan
    puff pastry, defrosted
    if frozen
plain flour, for dusting
plant-based milk or
    cream, for brushing
250g (9oz) baby carrots
virgin olive oil,
    for drizzling
salt and pepper

A lovely autumn or winter pie... Chunky chestnut mushrooms are surrounded with a nice deep silky sauce, followed by the crunch of the puff pastry. What's not to like? Tuck in and enjoy every mouthful.

Preheat the oven to 190°C (375°F), Gas Mark 5. Combine the dried porcini and measured water and set aside to soak for 15 minutes. Drain, reserving the soaking liquid. (The water is full of umami flavour and will help add depth to your sauce.) Squeeze out all the excess water from the porcini, then finely chop.

Heat 1 tablespoon of sunflower oil in a large frying pan over medium-high heat. Add the plant mince and cook for 3–5 minutes, until browned. Put it into a bowl and set aside.

Heat another tablespoon of sunflower oil in the same pan. Add the onions and sweat for 7 minutes, until translucent and softened. Add the garlic and chestnut mushrooms and cook for another 3 minutes. Stir in the flour. Pour in the stout and stock. Pour in the mushroom soaking liquid, leaving out any bits of grit.

Add 5 sprigs of thyme and 1 teaspoon of maple syrup. Season with salt and pepper, then gently simmer for 20 minutes, until thickened. Tip the sauce into an ovenproof dish and stir in the cooked plant mince.

Roll out the pastry on a lightly floured surface, large enough to fit over the dish. Lay it over the top of the stew, trimming away any excess pastry from the edges. Using a fork, crimp the edges to seal. Brush the top of the pastry with the milk and then make a few slits in the top of the pastry to avoid explosions in your oven! Bake for 30 minutes.

Place the carrots on a baking sheet. Drizzle over the remaining maple syrup and olive oil and toss to coat. Top with the remaining 2 thyme sprigs and roast for the final 10 minutes of baking time.

Serve the pie with the roasted maple carrots on the side. You'll be proper stoked.

GUEST CHEF·WICKED KITCHEN
BBQ PULLED
MUSHROOM SANDWICH
· SERVES 2 ·

6 large king oyster
    mushrooms
2 tablespoons sage, onion
    and garlic seasoning
    (see Note)
½ teaspoon granulated
    garlic
½ teaspoon black pepper
4 tablespoons sunflower
    or vegetable oil
225ml (8fl oz) your
    favourite BBQ sauce
3 tablespoons citrusy
    IPA beer
2 teaspoons Vegan Butter
    (see page 36)
2 soft burger buns
sliced jalapeño (optional)

NOTE
I use Wicked Kitchen Sage,
Onion & Garlic Seasoning.
If you can't find it, make
your own by mixing
together 1 tablespoon
granulated onion,
1½ teaspoons ground sage,
1½ teaspoons granulated
garlic, 1½ teaspoons sea
salt, 1 teaspoon ground
coriander, ¾ teaspoon
ground black pepper
and ½ teaspoon sugar.

Derek Sarno – chef and co-founder of Wicked Kitchen, cookbook author, animal lover, master of mushroom cookery and my friend – is a chef on a mission to help people make wicked delicious vegan food. He has also been known to train squirrels. According to Derek, 'You don't have to sacrifice your favourite backyard BBQ when you go vegan. Leave the animals alone and grab some 'shrooms instead. You might like this version better.' A vegan pulled mushroom sandwich, coming right up!

Preheat the oven to 200°C (400°F), Gas Mark 6. Line a baking sheet with baking paper.

Shred the mushrooms by holding the cap and running a fork lengthways along the stem, pulling away from the cap. Pull apart the shreds with your fingers and place into a large bowl. Thinly slice the caps, if necessary. Add the seasoning, granulated garlic and pepper and mix to coat.

Heat the oil in a large cast-iron pan over medium-high heat until it's ripping hot. Add the seasoned mushrooms and cook for 8–10 minutes, stirring occasionally, until browned all over.

Mix the BBQ sauce and beer in the same bowl used for the mushrooms. Add the cooked mushrooms back to the bowl and toss. Spread the sauced mushrooms on the prepared baking sheet. Roast for 10–15 minutes, until browned and caramelized. Stir halfway through for even browning.

Butter the inside of the buns. Place, cut side up, in the hot pan. Toast for 1–2 minutes, until toasted and golden brown.

Transfer the buns to plates. Pile the mushrooms onto the buns, then top with sliced jalapeño.

CHEESY POTATO BALLS
SERVES 4

For the potato balls
5 good-sized floury
   potatoes (King
   Edward), peeled
100g (3½oz) vegan
   cheese, grated
bunch of spring onions,
   chopped
3 tablespoons chickpea
   flour or plain flour,
   plus extra for coating
½ teaspoon garlic salt
pinch of chilli powder,
   or to taste
salt and pepper
your favourite dips,
   to serve

For the coating
liquid from 400g (14oz)
   can chickpeas
   (aquafaba)
panko breadcrumbs
plain flour

For the assembly
100g (3½oz) vegan
   cheese, cut into 1-cm
   (½-inch) cubes
sunflower oil, for
   deep-frying

These balls are great fun and would be great to serve at parties. You can make them big yet mouth-sized, so they pop easily into your mouth. Then, dip 'em in the sauce of your choosing. Garlic mayo? Sriracha? Maybe even a classic ketchup? Dip away and taste the vegan cheese ooze out at first bite.

Make the potato balls. Add 2cm (¾ inch) boiling water to a large saucepan. Place the potatoes in a steamer basket over the saucepan, then cover. Steam the potatoes for 20–25 minutes over a medium heat, until a knife can easily pierce the potato without resistance.

Using a potato ricer, mash the potatoes. Season with salt and pepper. Add the vegan cheese, spring onions, chickpea flour, garlic salt and chilli powder. Set aside to cool.

Make the coating. Place the flour, aquafaba, panko breadcrumbs in 3 separate bowls – and in that order, too.

To assemble, fill your hand with a nice bit of the potato mixture, about 3 rounded tablespoons. Shape into a ball, then flatten it out a little. Add a cube of vegan cheese in the centre. Wrap the potato mixture around the cheese to cover. Repeat with the remaining potato mixture and cheese cubes.

Dip a potato ball in the flour, the aquafaba and then the breadcrumbs. Put on a plate and repeat with the remaining potato mixture. Rest, uncovered, in the fridge for 15 minutes, until slightly chilled.

Heat the oil in a deep fryer or deep saucepan to 180°C (350°F), or until a cube of bread browns in 30 seconds. Remove the potato balls from the fridge and carefully lower them into the hot oil, working in batches to avoid overcrowding. Deep-fry the potato balls for 5 minutes, until golden brown. Using a slotted spoon, transfer them to a plate lined with kitchen paper to drain. Repeat with the remaining potato balls.

Serve immediately with your favourite dips!

THE ULTIMATE HANGOVER DIRTY FRIES

SERVES 2 GENEROUSLY

For the sauce
1 tablespoon olive oil
2 shallots, finely chopped
3 garlic cloves, crushed
400g (14oz) can
    chopped tomatoes
bunch of basil or
    oregano, chopped
1 teaspoon brown sugar
1 tablespoon balsamic glaze
salt and pepper

For the fries
1 litre (1¾ pints) sunflower
    oil, for deep-frying
4 large Maris Piper potatoes,
    cut into batons

For the assembly
1 tablespoon olive oil
2 vegan burger patties,
    broken into small chunks
60g (2¼oz) vegan lardons
4 spring onions, thinly sliced
1 red chilli, finely chopped
80g (2¾oz) finely sliced
    vegan cheese

You've had a massive night out and you're craving hangover food? I have the solution, these dirty fries are bangin'. Sure, it has a fair bit of processed foods, but who really cares when you're on the sofa suffering? And if you can't be arsed to make your own chips, then store-bought chips will do.

Preheat the oven to 200°C (400°F), Gas Mark 6.

Make the sauce. Heat the olive oil in a frying pan over medium heat. Add the shallots and garlic and sweat for 5 minutes, until softened. Add the tomatoes, basil (or oregano), sugar and balsamic glaze. Season with salt and pepper. Simmer for 5 minutes. Set aside.

Make the fries. Heat the sunflower oil in a deep fryer or deep saucepan to 180°C (350°F), or until a cube of bread browns in 30 seconds. Carefully lower the fries into the hot oil and deep-fry for 8–10 minutes, or until deeply golden. Tip the cooked fries onto a plate lined with kitchen paper to drain.

Heat the olive oil in a frying pan over medium-high heat. Add the chunks of vegan patties and the lardons and sauté for 5 minutes, until cooked.

Put the fries into an ovenproof dish. Top with the vegan patties and lardons, then tip in the tomato sauce. Sprinkle with half of the spring onions. Top with the chilli and vegan cheese. Bake for 15 minutes, until all the cheese is melted.

Garnish with the remaining spring onions. Now, let it give you that long-awaited hug while you melt into the couch and recover from last night's mayhem.

CREAMY ROAST GARLIC and TOMATO PASTA

SERVES 2

6 good-sized tomatoes, halved
2 sweet peppers, halved
olive oil, for drizzling
1 garlic bulb
200g (7oz) spaghetti
    or your choice of pasta
15g (½oz) basil leaves
2 tablespoons nutritional yeast
125ml (4fl oz) plant-based
    cream (I used oat)
a dash of chilli sauce,
    or to taste
salt and pepper

To garnish (optional)
chopped basil
chilli flakes

This simple roast garlic and tomato recipe is the best. The recipe serves two, so this is a good dish to make when you're having a date or friend over. In fact, if you prepared it for a date, let me know if they were impressed!

Preheat the oven to 200°C (400°F), Gas Mark 6.

Place the tomatoes and sweet peppers on a baking sheet and lightly drizzle with oil. Slice a few millimetres off the top of the garlic bulb so you can just see a little flesh of the garlic cloves inside their papery skins. Wrap it in kitchen foil and place it on the baking sheet. Roast for 30–35 minutes, until the vegetables are softened.

Meanwhile, cook the pasta according to packet instructions. Don't drain the water from the pasta.

Transfer the roasted vegetables to a food processor. Squeeze the garlic cloves into the bowl of the food processor, then add the basil, nutritional yeast and plant-based cream. Add any juice from the baking sheet and blitz until smooth.

Pour the sauce into a saucepan and bring to a simmer. Add the chilli sauce, then season to taste with salt and pepper.

Using kitchen tongs, pick up the spaghetti from the water and add to the sauce. (Some of the pasta water will come along with it but that's cool.) Stir well to mix.

Transfer to a serving plate, then add chopped basil and/or chilli flakes, if using.

'TOFISH' and CHIPPIES

SERVES 4

1 litre (1¾ pints)
   sunflower
   oil, for deep-frying
1kg (2lb 4oz) Maris
   Piper potatoes,
   cut into batons
450g (1lb) firm tofu
4 large nori sheets
65g (2¼oz) self-raising
   flour
1 teaspoon salt
1 teaspoon garlic powder
1 teaspoon ground
   turmeric
300ml (10fl oz) water
1 tablespoon vegan
   fish sauce

To serve
1 lemon, cut into wedges
mushy peas (optional)

Friday night is CHIPPIES night in my house! Before I became vegan, way back in 2015, I used to love a piece of battered cod with my chips. Since turning vegan, I've always wanted a substitute. A piece of tofu topped with a slice of nori evokes a taste of the sea – the seaweed 'fish skin' really works a treat AND it's full of plant protein.

Heat the oil in a deep fryer or deep saucepan to 180°C (350°F), or until a cube of bread browns in 30 seconds. Carefully lower the potatoes into the hot oil and deep-fry 8–10 minutes, or until deeply golden.

Meanwhile, prepare your 'tofish'. Use a tofu press to extract all the water from the tofu. (If you don't have one to hand, wrap the tofu in kitchen paper and place some pressure on it to extract the excess water.) Cut the tofu into 4 thick slices.

Cut the nori sheets to the same size of the tofu. Trim it to look like fish skin. This will give it that taste of the sea.

In a bowl, combine the flour, salt, garlic powder and turmeric and mix. Stir in the measured water and vegan fish sauce and mix well.

Tip the cooked chips onto a plate lined with kitchen paper to drain. Transfer to a roasting pan and keep hot in a warm oven. Keep the oil heated as you'll need it for the 'tofish'.

Coat the 'tofish' in the batter. Carefully lower them into the hot oil and deep-fry for 6–8 minutes, until the batter turns a nice golden brown. Using a slotted spoon, transfer the 'tofish' to a plate lined with kitchen paper.

Now it's time to serve. Plate up the 'tofish' and chips. Don't forget to serve with lemon wedges and mushy peas, if you like.

GNOCCHI WITH BASIL *and* SAGE PESTO

SERVES 2

For the pesto
40g (1½oz) pine nuts
50g (1¾oz) nutritional
    yeast
50g (1¾oz) basil leaves
25g (1oz) sage leaves
1 garlic clove
2 tablespoons lemon juice
75ml (2½fl oz) extra
    virgin olive oil
salt and pepper

For the gnocchi
400g (14oz) potatoes
25g (1oz) flour,
    preferably '00' flour,
    plus extra for dusting
virgin olive oil, for frying

*Potatoes are so versatile, I love them. These fluffy, little pillows
of goodness are coated in a deliciously vibrant sauce.*

Make the pesto. Heat a small frying pan over medium-high heat.
Add the pine nuts and toast for 2–3 minutes, until fragrant. In a food
processor, combine the pine nuts and remaining ingredients, except
for the olive oil. Blitz until roughly chopped. With the motor running,
gradually pour in the oil and pulse into a pesto consistency. Set aside.

Make the gnocchi. Put the potatoes in a saucepan of water and bring
to a boil. Cook for 10 minutes, or until they can be easily pierced with
a knife without resistance. Drain, then push the potatoes through a
potato ricer to guarantee a smooth mash. Add half the flour. Mix well.

Dust your work surface with flour. Transfer the potato mixture onto
the surface and knead together (not for too long though, as you'll
work the gluten and create tough gnocchi). Divide the mix into 4 balls.
Roll one ball into a rope, about 15mm (⅝ inch) in diameter. The mixture
is fragile, so work carefully. Cut the rope into 2.5-cm (1-inch) segments.
Repeat with the remaining dough. Roll the gnocchi pieces along the
back of a fork to create ridges, which helps them pick up more sauce,
then transfer to the fridge for an hour or so to firm up.

When ready to cook, bring a saucepan of water to a boil. Working in
batches, carefully lower the gnocchi into the water. Cook for 1–2 minutes,
until they rise to the surface. Using a slotted spoon, scoop them out,
draining all the water, and place on a plate. Repeat with the rest.

Heat 2 tablespoons of olive oil in a frying pan over medium-high
heat. Add the gnocchi and fry until golden. Transfer to a plate and
repeat with the remaining gnocchi, adding more oil if necessary.

Place all the gnocchi back into the pan, add the pesto and cook
until warmed through.

Transfer to a serving plate and serve.

FLY-AWAY CAULIFLOWER BUFFALO BITES

SERVES 2

For the battered cauliflower
150g (5½oz) vegan Greek yogurt
2 tablespoons plant-based milk
1 tablespoon onion powder
1 tablespoon garlic powder
½ teaspoon smoked paprika
1 cauliflower, broken into
  large florets (see Note)
salt and pepper

For the buffalo sauce
2 tablespoons Vegan Butter
  (see page 36)
7 tablespoons hot sauce
1 teaspoon maple syrup
1 teaspoon liquid smoke
  (optional)
2½ tablespoons chickpea flour

For the dip
100g (3½oz) vegan Greek yogurt
1 teaspoon Dijon mustard
1 teaspoon maple syrup
1 teaspoon cider vinegar
¼ teaspoon garlic powder
½ teaspoon smoked paprika
2 tablespoons chives,
  chopped (optional)
salt and pepper

NOTE
Discarded cauliflower leaves
can be kept in the fridge and
cooked like cabbage.

This is a nice little starter or snack.

Preheat the oven to 220°C (425°F), Gas Mark 7. Line a large baking sheet with baking paper.

Make the battered cauliflower. In a large bowl, combine all the ingredients, except the cauliflower, and mix well. Generously season with salt and pepper. Chuck in the florets and mix until coated. (Make sure the batter seeps into the crevices of the florets for mega coverage.) Spread out the florets onto the baking sheet. Bake for 15 minutes. Turn them over, then bake for another 15 minutes.

Meanwhile, make the buffalo sauce. Combine all the ingredients in a small saucepan. Heat over medium-high heat, until the vegan butter has melted and the chickpea flour has dissolved.

Transfer the sauce to a large bowl. Add the cauliflower wings and toss to evenly coat. Tip them back onto the baking sheet and bake for another 5 minutes.

Make the dip. Combine all the ingredients in a bowl.

You're ready to rock. Put the cauliflower wings in a good-sized bowl. Serve them hot with the dip.

BAKED SWEET POTATO WITH BEAN and CHILLI SLAW

SERVES 4

4 good-sized sweet potatoes
4 generous tablespoons Vegan
 Butter (see page 36)

For the slaw
2 green chillies, finely chopped
2 spring onions, thinly sliced
1 red pepper, cored, deseeded
 and thinly sliced
1 carrot, grated
½ white cabbage, shredded
½ red cabbage, shredded
200g (7oz) black-eyed beans
5 tablespoons vegan mayonnaise
2 tablespoons lemon juice
1 tablespoon maple syrup
1 teaspoon cider vinegar
1 teaspoon Dijon mustard
salt and pepper

Tasty, crunchy slaw is everything. It can top a baked sweet spud, as shown in this recipe, fill a sandwich or burger or be served on its own. A mandoline helps to finely cut cabbage, peppers and spring onions, but you need to be extremely careful when using it. I suggest you use a knife if you have decent knife skills.

Preheat the oven to 180°C (350°F), Gas Mark 4.

Prick the sweet potatoes all over with a fork or sharp knife. Place them on the top shelf of the oven and bake for 40–50 minutes, until a knife can easily pierce them without resistance.

Meanwhile, make the slaw. In a large bowl, combine all the vegetables and beans and toss well.

In a small bowl, combine the mayo, lemon juice, maple syrup, cider vinegar and mustard. Mix well and dress your slaw. Season to taste with salt and pepper.

Plate your sweet spuds and cut a cross into each one. Add a knob of vegan butter, then top with the slaw. Mmmmmmm!

NACHOS

SERVES 4–6

For the tomato salsa
200g (7oz) cherry
   tomatoes, quartered
½ red onion, finely chopped
½ garlic clove, grated
bunch of coriander,
   finely chopped
1 tablespoon lime juice
salt and pepper

For the cashew cream
100g (3½oz) cashew nuts,
   soaked overnight
1½ tablespoons nutritional yeast
½ teaspoon garlic powder
½ teaspoon red or white
   miso paste
100ml (3½fl oz) plant-based milk
salt and pepper

For the assembly
200g (7oz) tortilla chips
3–5 jarred jalapeño peppers
2 spring onions, chopped

Dan Joyce, who was part of the Dirty Sanchez *crew, used to love his nachos. Whenever he saw them on a menu at a restaurant, he would order them. This a good dish when you have group of mates coming over and you don't have a lot of time to spend in the kitchen. The key is to soak the cashews the night before, so the dish come together super quickly before everyone walks through the door.*

Make your tomato salsa. In a bowl, combine all the ingredients. Set aside.

Make the cashew cream. Drain the cashews. In a food processor, combine all the ingredients and blitz until smooth and creamy.

Place the tortilla chips in a bowl or serving dish. Add the salsa, then pour over your cashew cream. Top with jalapeños and spring onions. Tuck in.

CHAPTER
3

30
MINUTES
TO A
BANGING
MEAL

EASY PEASY TOMATO SAUCE WITH PASTA 66

'THE DUNNER' PIZZA 68

BOUNCY BEAN BALLS 69

RAINBOW-COLOURED STIR-FRY 70

WILD MUSHROOM AND MIXED PEPPER FAJITAS 72

EASY DHAL WITH CHAPATIS 74

EASY, CREAMY, PEASY AND ASPARAGUS-Y PASTA 78

VEGETABLE FRIED RICE 80

MISO NOODLE SOUP 82

BROCCOLI AND ASPARAGUS WITH CREAMY
AVOCADO DRESSING 83

IT AIN'T TRICKY – A COUSCOUS QUICKIE 84

VEGETABLE FRITTERZ 86

BURRITO BOWLS 87

We all have such crazy busy lives these days that having no time to focus on food is always an issue. Most of us don't want to bung a microwave meal into the popty ping (only for it to come out hot enough to burn your mouth off).

So, to help you all out, this chapter has plenty of delicious 30-minute meals that won't eat into your busy schedule.

EASY PEASY TOMATO SAUCE WITH PASTA

SERVES 4

For the Easy Peasy Tomato Sauce
olive oil, for frying
2 shallots, chopped
3 garlic cloves, chopped
400g (14oz) cherry tomatoes
1 tablespoon brown sugar
3 tablespoons tomato purée
dash of balsamic vinegar
500g (1lb 2oz) passata
30g (1oz) basil leaves, chopped
salt and pepper

To serve
400g (14oz) pasta of your choice
vegan hard cheese, grated
   (optional)

Like a lot of us these days, I have a busy schedule. And I can appreciate quick and easy meals that can be prepared in a matter of minutes. So whenever I make a tomato sauce, I also double up and bung a batch in the fridge of freezer, perfect for those times when I need a carb hit, before I head to the gym or go for a run or cycle. This one's a smasher.

Cook the pasta according to packet instructions. Set aside.

Make the Easy Peasy Tomato Sauce: heat a little olive oil in a frying pan over medium heat. Add the shallots and sweat for 5 minutes, until softened. Add the garlic and tomatoes and fry for another 3 minutes. Stir in the sugar, tomato purée and balsamic and cook off for 5 minutes. Add the passata and bring to a simmer. Stir in the basil and pasta. Season with salt and pepper.

Serve it up with grated vegan hard cheese, if liked.

'THE DUNNER' PIZZA
· SERVES 2 ·

2 teaspoons olive oil,
   plus extra for brushing
½ red onion, chopped
½ red pepper, cored,
   deseeded and thinly sliced
½ small courgette, thinly sliced
handful of mushrooms,
   trimmed and sliced
2 large soft flour tortillas
2 pinches of garlic powder
60g (2¼oz) Easy Peasy Tomato
   Sauce (see page 66)
2 large handfuls of shredded
   vegan mozzarella
2 pinches of dried oregano
salt and pepper

To garnish (optional)
handful of rocket leaves
vegan Parmesan cheese,
   for sprinkling

When I began to think of 30-minute recipe ideas for this book, I thought of my fiancée's quick pizza. I was (half-heartedly) minding my own business, when I noticed her cooking something. When I asked what the hell she was making, she replied with 'a pizza'. Honestly, it's the first time I'd ever seen a pizza made like that. However, if you're a fan of wafer-thin pizzas and a simple low-calorie meal, then this is for you. She was kind enough to share it below. You can use any type of vegetable for this. Just make sure to cook them first.

Preheat the oven to 200°C (400°F), Gas Mark 6.

Heat the oil in a frying pan over medium heat. Add the onion, red pepper, courgette and mushrooms. Sweat for 3 minutes, until softened.

Place the tortillas on a large baking sheet, then brush each with oil. Sprinkle with the garlic powder, salt, and pepper. Bake for 3 minutes, or until golden.

Spread the tomato sauce on top, then arrange the veggies on top. Sprinkle with vegan mozzarella. Bake for 4 minutes, until the cheese has melted.

Sprinkle the oregano over the cheese, add the rocket and vegan Parmesan, if using. Slice and enjoy!

BOUNCY BEAN BALLS

MAKES ABOUT 14

Easy Peasy Tomato Sauce
   (see page 66)
salt and pepper
your choice of pasta,
   to serve

For the bean balls
1 tablespoon ground flaxseed
2½ tablespoons water
200g (7oz) canned red kidney
   beans, drained and rinsed
100g (3½oz) white rice,
   cooked and cooled
2 tablespoons oat flour
2 tablespoons nutritional yeast
2 tablespoons Italian seasoning
2 garlic cloves
2 tablespoons red miso paste
1 tablespoon tomato paste

To garnish (optional)
chopped basil
vegan Parmesan cheese

*This is an ace way to put the easy tomato sauce to use.
I simmer these bean balls in the sauce, then serve them
over spaghetti or any type of pasta I might have on hand.
They are dead good. First, you'll need to make a flax egg,
which helps to bind the bean balls together.*

Preheat the oven to 180°C (350°F), Gas Mark 4. Line a
baking sheet with baking paper.

Make the bean balls. In a small bowl, combine the flaxseed
and measured water. Mix well, then set aside for 5 minutes.

In a food processor, combine all the bean ball ingredients,
including your flax egg, and mix for 3–4 minutes, until it
comes together like a stiff paste.

Wet your hands, then form the paste into small balls,
about 2cm (¾ inch) in diameter. Place them on the prepared
baking sheet and bake for 5 minutes, until cooked through.
Set aside to cool.

Meanwhile, now's the time to cook the pasta according
to packet instructions.

Heat the tomato sauce in a large saucepan over medium
heat. Add the bean balls and simmer for 10 minutes until
warmed through.

Garnish with chopped basil and/or Parmesan and serve
with the pasta.

RAINBOW-COLOURED STIR-FRY

SERVES 2

For the marinated tempeh
2 garlic cloves, crushed
2.5-cm (1-inch) piece of fresh
  root ginger, finely chopped
1 tablespoon cornflour
½ tablespoon rice vinegar
pinch of chilli flakes
4 tablespoons soy sauce
100ml (3½fl oz) vegetable stock
1 teaspoon toasted sesame oil
200g (7oz) tempeh, cut into
  bite-sized pieces

For the stir-fry
virgin olive oil, for frying
¼ red cabbage, shredded
½ red pepper, cored, deseeded
  and cut into strips
½ yellow pepper, cored,
  deseeded and cut
  into strips
½ head of broccoli,
  cut into florets
1 carrot, thinly sliced
  into matchsticks
80g (2¾oz) baby corn
80g (2¾oz) mangetout
steamed rice, to serve (optional)

If you want an easy, full-flavoured meal in 20 minutes or less, then this is it. This stir-fry makes a quick and tasty option after a long day of work, cycling or training, plus it's packed with protein-rich tempeh. The veg should have a nice crunch for texture, so be sure not to overcook it. I prepare this stir-fry in a wok; however, you can use a frying pan as well. Fun fact: Chinese–American chef Ken Hom introduced the wok to the UK more than 30 years ago.

Make the marinated tempeh. In a bowl, combine all the ingredients, except for the tempeh, and mix well. Add the tempeh, cover with clingfilm and refrigerate for at least 15 minutes but preferably overnight (to allow the tempeh to really soak up the flavours).

Now's the time to cook your rice, if using, according to packet instructions.

Make the stir-fry. Heat 2 tablespoons of olive oil in a wok or frying pan over medium-high heat. Using a slotted spoon, add the tempeh into the pan. (Reserve the marinade for later.) Sear for 5–10 minutes, until golden on all sides. Transfer to a bowl and set aside.

Heat another tablespoon of oil in the wok. Chuck in all the veg and stir-fry for 5 minutes. Add the tempeh and reserved marinade and fry for another 3 minutes. Transfer to a serving plate.

Serve on its own or with steamed rice.

WILD MUSHROOM and MIXED PEPPER FAJITAS

SERVES 6

For the salsa
2 tomatoes, finely chopped
1 red onion, finely chopped
1 green chilli, finely chopped
½ garlic clove, grated
20g (¾oz) coriander,
    finely chopped
2 tablespoons lime juice
1 teaspoon balsamic vinegar
dash of extra virgin olive oil
salt and pepper

For the guacamole
2 ripe avocados
2 tablespoons lime juice
salt and pepper

For the fajitas
virgin olive oil, for frying
3 garlic cloves, thinly sliced
1 red onion, thinly sliced
½ red pepper, cored, deseeded
    and thickly sliced
½ green pepper, cored, deseeded
    and thickly sliced
½ yellow pepper, cored,
    deseeded and thickly sliced
150g (5½oz) porcini mushrooms,
    thickly sliced
25g (1oz) packet of taco
    seasoning mix
6 soft tortillas
6 tablespoons vegan yogurt

The first time I had fajitas was for a birthday meal at TGI Friday's when I was a kid. Back in the late eighties, when the chain was introduced to the UK, it was THE place to go (at least, for us kids). Fajitas happen to be one of the many dishes we assume to originate in Mexico but are, in actuality, American or Tex-Mex. Either way, this is a simple yet tasty dish: spice 'em up, then wrap and eat 'em.

Make the salsa. In a small bowl, combine all the ingredients and set aside.

Make the guacamole. Mash the avocados in a bowl, using a fork or a potato masher. Add the lime juice, then season with salt and pepper. Set it next to the salsa.

Heat 2 tablespoons of oil in a large frying pan over medium-high heat. Add the garlic, onion, peppers and mushrooms and sauté for 5 minutes. Add the taco seasoning and a bit of water according to packet instructions. Fry for 5 minutes.

Heat a frying pan over medium heat. Add a tortilla and heat for a few seconds on each side, until warmed up and softened. Transfer to a plate, then repeat with the remaining tortillas.

It's time to build up your fajitas. Spread a bit of guac on each tortilla. Add your veggies, then top with salsa and a dollop of yogurt. Fold up the fajita and you're good to go.

EASY DHAL WITH CHAPATIS

SERVES 2

For the chapatis
200g (7oz) '00' flour,
    plus extra for dusting
large pinch of salt
100ml (3½fl oz) water
1 tablespoon olive oil

For the dhal
2 tablespoons coriander seeds
2 teaspoons cumin seeds
2 teaspoons ground turmeric
1 teaspoon garam masala
1 onion, finely chopped
5 garlic cloves, finely chopped
2.5-cm (1-inch) piece of fresh
    root ginger, finely chopped
400g (14oz) can brown lentils,
    rinsed and drained
100ml (3½fl oz) vegetable stock
400ml (14fl oz) coconut milk
2–4 chillies, finely chopped,
    plus sliced extra to serve
coriander, to garnish (optional)

I go for this dhal when I'm pressed for time because I can bash it out in under 30 minutes. It's amazing with homemade chapatis, but if you're in a hurry, serve the dhal with store-bought flatbreads instead.

Make the chapatis. In a large bowl, combine all the ingredients and mix until it forms a dough and the sides of the bowl are free of flour. Knead the dough until smooth. Place in a bowl and cover with clingfilm or a tea towel. Set aside to rest for 30 minutes.

Make the dhal. Heat a frying pan over high heat. Add the coriander and cumin seeds and toast for 2–3 minutes, until fragrant. (Be sure not to burn them.) Transfer the seeds to a spice grinder or a pestle and mortar and grind to a powder. Stir in the turmeric and garam masala.

In the same pan, heat a tablespoon of oil over medium-high heat. Add the onion, reduce the heat to medium-low and sweat for 10 minutes, until softened and browned. Add the garlic and ginger and cook for 2–3 minutes. Add the spices and cook until fragrant. If it seems too dry, add a few tablespoons of water. Again, do not burn the spices as your dhal will taste awful.

Add the lentils, stock and coconut milk to the mixture and stir. Add the chillies and bring it to a boil. Reduce the heat to medium-low, cover and simmer for 10 minutes, stirring occasionally.

Meanwhile, place the chapati dough on a floured work surface and divide into 6 pieces. Roll each into a ball.

Heat a frying pan over medium-high heat. Roll out a chapati into a thin, flat disk and add to the hot pan. Dry-fry for 30–45 seconds, until it's blistered and slightly charred. Flip over and cook for another minute. Transfer to a plate, then cover with a tea towel to keep warm. Repeat with the remaining chapatis.

To serve, transfer the dhal to a serving bowl, then sprinkle with sliced chilli and coriander, if using. Serve with the warm chapatis, made for mopping up all that spicy creamy deliciousness.

EASY, CREAMY, PEASY and ASPARAGUS~Y PASTA

SERVES 2

200g (7oz) your choice of pasta
125g (4½oz) asparagus,
  trimmed and halved
  widthways (see Note)
2 garlic cloves
1 avocado
100g (3½oz) vegan cream cheese
2 tablespoons nutritional yeast
50ml (2fl oz) plant-based milk
  (oat, almond or cashew)
100g (3½oz) petit pois
salt and pepper

NOTE
The easiest way to trim an
asparagus is to bend it in half
until it breaks. It snaps at the
perfect point.

Keep this recipe for the asparagus season (late February to June in the UK) and enjoy the creamy green goodness.

Cook the pasta according to packet instructions.

Meanwhile, bring a saucepan of water to a boil. Add the asparagus and cook for 3–4 minutes, until just tender. (Do not overcook the asparagus; otherwise, it turns stringy and fibrous and unpleasant to eat.) Drain, then set aside.

In a food processor, combine the garlic, avocado, vegan cream cheese, nutritional yeast and plant-based milk. Blitz until smooth.

Pour the sauce into a saucepan and bring to a simmer. Season with salt and pepper. Add the peas, asparagus and pasta to the sauce. Mix until the pasta is well coated.

Transfer to plates and serve with a good grinding of black pepper.

VEGETABLE FRIED RICE

SERVES 4

For the seasoning sauce
1 tablespoon soy sauce
1 tablespoon rice vinegar
1 tablespoon toasted sesame oil

For the fried rice
200g (7oz) white or brown rice
virgin olive oil, for frying
½ red onion, chopped
3 garlic cloves, finely chopped
2.5-cm (1-inch) piece of fresh
    root ginger, finely chopped
1 red pepper, cored, deseeded
    and chopped
1 cob of sweetcorn, kernels
    shaven off, or 100g (3½oz)
    frozen sweetcorn
100g (3½oz) Tenderstem
    broccoli, trimmed and
    chopped into short lengths
100g (3½oz) shiitake
    mushrooms, sliced
200g (7oz) defrosted peas
100g (3½oz) cashew nuts
handful of chia seeds
1 lime, halved
2 spring onions, shredded

Simple, quick and easy veg and rice.

Make the seasoning sauce. Mix the ingredients together in a small bowl.

Make the fried rice. Cook your rice according to packet instructions.

Heat 2 tablespoons of olive oil in a wok or frying pan over medium-high heat. Add the onion and sweat for 7 minutes, until softened. Add the garlic and ginger and sweat for 2 minutes. Stir in the seasoning sauce. Add the pepper, sweetcorn, Tenderstem broccoli and mushrooms. Fry for 3 minutes until cooked.

Mix in the drained and cooked rice, peas, cashews and chia seeds. Add the juice from half a lime into the pan.

Transfer the fried rice to a large plate. Garnish with the spring onions. Cut the remaining half of the lime into wedges and add to the plate. Serve.

MISO NOODLE SOUP

SERVES 6

100g (3½oz) edamame beans
virgin olive oil, for frying
1 onion, finely chopped
5 garlic cloves, minced
2.5-cm (1-inch) piece of
    fresh root ginger, minced
200g (7oz) mushrooms,
    trimmed and thinly sliced
200g (7oz) carrot,
    finely chopped
100g (3½oz) baby sweetcorn,
    halved lengthways
1.3 litres (2¼ pints)
    vegetable stock
1 tablespoon red or white
    miso paste
50g (1¾oz) dried rice noodles
salt and pepper

To garnish
2 spring onions, thinly sliced
black sesame seeds
broccoli sprouts (optional)

This book is all about easy meals and its doesn't get easier than this soup. Not only is it quick but it's also very easy, you just put it all into the pot. When cooked in only 20 minutes time, you'll have a delicious soup with nice long stringy rice noodles.

If the edamame beans are frozen, then pour some boiling water over them to defrost. Drain.

Heat 1 tablespoon of oil in a frying pan over medium-high heat. Add the onion and sweat for 7 minutes. Add the garlic and ginger and cook for another 2 minutes.

Add the mushrooms, carrot, sweetcorn and edamame. Pour in the stock, then stir in the miso.

Add the rice noodles and bring to a boil. Reduce the heat to medium-low and simmer for 5 minutes, stirring occasionally. Season with salt and pepper.

Ladle the soup and noodles into bowls. Garnish with the spring onions, sesame seeds and broccoli sprouts, if using.

BROCCOLI *and* ASPARAGUS WITH CREAMY AVOCADO DRESSING

SERVES 2

325g (11½oz) Tenderstem
 broccoli, trimmed
250g (9oz) asparagus,
 trimmed (see Note)
Creamy Avocado Dressing
 (see page 141)

To garnish
a handful pine nuts
chilli flakes, for sprinkling

NOTE
The easiest way to trim an
asparagus is to bend it in half
until it breaks. It snaps at the
perfect point.

This simple and delicious dish whips up super-fast. I even went a bit posh by using Tenderstem instead of ordinary broccoli. (Ha!)

Bring a medium saucepan of water to a boil. Add the Tenderstem broccoli and cook for 5 minutes, until they're tender but still have a bite. Using tongs, transfer the broccoli to a plate. Add the asparagus and cook for 3–4 minutes, until tender. Do not overcook the asparagus as it becomes limp and unpleasant. Transfer to the same plate.

Add the pine nuts and toast for 2–3 minutes, until fragrant and the oils are released.

Serve up the broccoli and asparagus, drizzle with the creamy avocado dressing and top with pine nuts. For a real kick, sprinkle with chilli flakes.

IT AIN'T TRICKY ~ A COUSCOUS QUICKIE

SERVES 2 GENEROUSLY OR 4 AS A SIDE

250g (9oz) couscous
250ml (9fl oz) hot
  vegetable stock
5 spring onions, finely sliced
2 tomatoes, chopped
1 small cucumber, chopped
1 yellow pepper, cored,
  deseeded and chopped
100g (3½oz) black or Kalamata
  olives, chopped
100g (3½oz) flat-leaf parsley,
  finely chopped
Maple-Mustard Dressing
  (see page 141)

Short of time for lunch or dinner? A couscous quickie is just what you want.

In a bowl, combine the couscous and vegetable stock. Cover and set aside for 10 minutes. Fluff up with a fork.

Add the spring onions, tomatoes, cucumber, pepper, olives and parsley. Drizzle with maple-mustard dressing.

And there you have it.

VEGETABLE FRITTERZ
SERVES 2

For the fritters
1 tablespoon chia seeds
5 tablespoons water
2–3 carrots, coarsely grated
1 courgette, coarsely grated
1 garlic clove, grated
50g (1¾oz) chickpea flour
½ teaspoon chilli powder
½ teaspoon ground cumin
½ teaspoon paprika
sunflower oil, for frying
3 spring onions, finely sliced
salt and pepper

For the harissa mayo
7 tablespoons vegan mayo
1 tablespoons harissa paste
½ garlic clove, grated

Whether you're using what's left in your fridge or you've purposely gone and bought the ingredients to make up a good batch of fritterz, this is a great way to enjoy vegetables – crispy on the outside and soft in the middle.

Make the fritters. In a small bowl, combine the chia seeds and 3 tablespoons of water. Set aside for 5 minutes, until it has a slimy texture (also known as chia eggs).

Meanwhile, place the grated carrots and courgette in the centre of a tea towel, then wring out the towel to remove the liquid. Place the grated veg in a large bowl.

Add the garlic, chickpea flour and spices. Add the remaining 2 tablespoons of water, the chia egg and season generously with salt and pepper. Mix together well.

Shape a ball of mixture in your hands and flatten it out into a fritter, about 1cm (½ inch) thick. Repeat with the remaining mixture.

Heat 3 tablespoons of oil in a large frying pan over medium-high heat. Working in batches, add the fritters and shallow fry for 3–5 minutes, until golden. Flip over, then fry for another 2 minutes. Transfer the fritters to a plate lined with kitchen paper. Repeat with the remaining fritters. (Alternatively, you can prepare them in an air fryer by air-frying them for a couple of minutes.)

Meanwhile, make your harissa mayo. Combine all the ingredients in a bowl and mix well.

Scatter the fritters with the sliced spring onion and dip away.

BURRITO BOWLS

SERVES 2

For the seasoning
1 teaspoon ground cumin
1 teaspoon smoked paprika
1 teaspoon chilli powder
salt and pepper

For the burrito bowls
1 avocado, diced
1 garlic clove, grated
½ red onion, finely chopped
½ red pepper, cored, deseeded
    and finely chopped
400g (14oz) can black beans,
    drained and rinsed
200g (7oz) can sweetcorn,
    drained and rinsed
200g (7oz) tomatoes,
    finely chopped
small bunch of coriander,
    finely chopped
100g (3½oz) microwave rice
2 generous dollops of
    vegan yogurt
½ teaspoon chipotle paste
2 lime wedges

*Here, spicy coated beans are served over a heaped bowl
of steamed rice. What does that mean? A satisfying meal
in next to no time.*

Make the seasoning. Combine all the ingredients in
a small bowl. Season generously with salt and pepper.

Make the burrito bowls. In a bowl, combine the avocado,
garlic, onion, red pepper, black beans, sweetcorn and
tomatoes. Sprinkle in the seasoning. Reserve a quarter
of the coriander, then add the rest to the bowl. Mix well.
Adjust the seasoning to taste.

Cook your microwave rice according to packet instructions.

In a small bowl, combine the vegan yogurt and chipotle.

Divide the cooked rice between 2 bowls. Add the bean
mixture, then a dollop of yogurt sauce to each. Sprinkle
with coriander, squeeze over a little lime juice and devour!

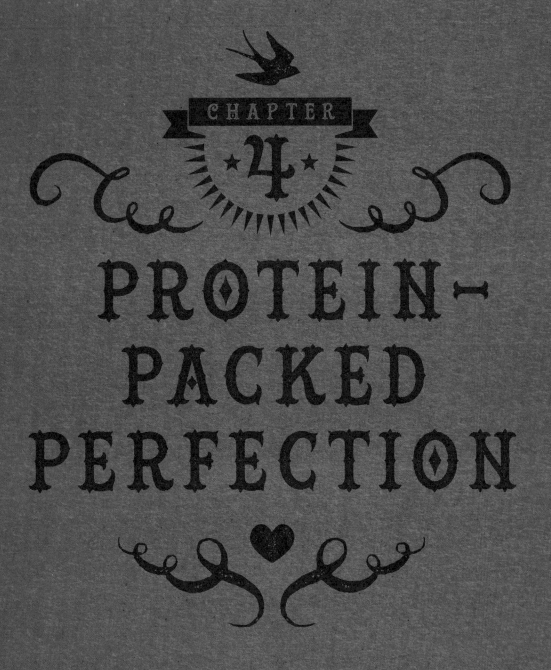

CHAPTER

4

PROTEIN-
PACKED
PERFECTION

It's great to see so many people taking up some kind of exercise these days, whether that is going to the gym, swimming, cycling, running, skateboarding or whatever, the list is endless. After participating in these activities, we always go in search of some good proteins to help fix our muscles. This chapter is full of high-protein recipes just for you. So next time someone says 'Where do you get your protein from?' then just show them this chapter!

MAKE YOUR OWN TOFU
MAKES 225G (8OZ)

200g (7oz) organic
    soy beans
3 litres (5¼ pints) water
125ml (4fl oz) lemon juice

NOTES

A tofu press is perfect for draining. If you don't have one to hand, wrap the tofu in kitchen paper and place some pressure on it to extract the excess water.

You can make double the quantity to yield around 450g (1lb) of tofu.

Some things in life are worth the wait. Making your own tofu takes a bloody while but its satisfaction is ten out of ten. You'll need a muslin and tofu press for this recipe. Be sure to keep the leftover soy pulp after it's been pressed, it can be added to smoothies, patties, pancakes, etc.

Put the soy beans in a bowl, cover with 1 litre (1¾ pints) of water and set aside overnight, until doubled in size. Rinse well, then add to a food blender with 2 litres (3½ pints) of water. Blend until smooth (in two batches if necessary, mixing half the beans and water in each batch).

Pour the mixture into a large saucepan and heat over high heat, stirring continuously. (Do not leave the pan unattended.) Bring to a boil, until the foamy head quickly rises. Take the pan off the heat for a few seconds, then reduce the heat to very low. Cook for another 15 minutes.

Place a muslin over a colander with a bowl underneath to catch the milk. Pour the mixture into the lined colander, then squeeze the muslin bag to extract all the 'milk' out of the mixture. (The solids remaining in the muslin bag is the soy pulp that can be used as mentioned above.)

Pour the milk into a clean saucepan. Stir constantly over medium-low heat, until warmed through and a little steam rises. Do NOT bring it up to a simmer. Stir in the lemon juice in a figure of '8' (it will curdle, that's fine). Take the pan off the heat and set aside, uncovered, for 15 minutes.

Line the colander again with muslin and place over a bowl, then spoon all the curdled tofu into the muslin. (If the curds are too small to be scooped with a spoon, pour the mixture through the muslin and set aside to drain.) Gently press down to remove excess water, then transfer the curd-filled muslin into a tofu press. Cover with more muslin, then the lid. Place a few cans on top to add a little pressure. Press for 15 minutes.

Take out the tofu, then carefully remove the muslin. Transfer the tofu to a container filled with cold water and set aside for 20 minutes to firm up. Your homemade tofu is now ready for use. Homemade tofu can be covered in water and stored in the fridge for up to 4 days. Replenish the water daily. The tofu can also be frozen, then defrosted before use. The texture will be crumblier.

✦ ✦✦ THREE TOFU IDEAS ✦ ✦✦
★

*Now that you've gone to the trouble of lovingly crafting your own tofu,
here are three ideas to enjoy the fruits of your labour.*

PREP 10 MINUTES ★ COOK 10 MINUTES

SALT and PEPPER TOFU
SERVES 2

For the salt and pepper tofu
1 litre (1¾ pints) sunflower
    oil, for deep-frying
    and frying
2 tablespoons cornflour
280g (10oz) firm tofu,
    drained and cut into
    2.5-cm (1-inch) cubes
1 teaspoon caster sugar
1 teaspoon white pepper
1 teaspoon five spice
½ teaspoon Sichuan pepper
½ onion, finely chopped
2 garlic cloves,
    finely chopped
1 red chilli, chopped
½ red pepper, cored,
    deseeded and chopped
steamed rice, to serve
    (optional)

For the dipping sauce
3 tablespoons soy sauce
1 tablespoon maple syrup
1 teaspoon toasted
    sesame oil
¼ shallot, finely chopped
½ red chilli, finely chopped

*When my fiancée told me to make salt and pepper tofu for the book,
I wasn't convinced. It wasn't something I had ever tried or would
expect to like but how wrong I was. It tastes incredible – enjoy!*

Cook your rice, if using, according to packet instructions.

Make the salt and pepper tofu. Heat the oil in a deep saucepan
to 190°C (375°F), or until a cube of bread browns in 30 seconds.

Tip the cornflour onto a plate. Add the tofu and toss to coat.
Lower the tofu into the hot oil and deep-fry for 3–4 minutes, until
crispy and golden. (Alternatively, shallow-fry for 5 minutes.)
Transfer the tofu to a plate lined with kitchen paper to drain.

Meanwhile, in a small bowl, combine the sugar, white pepper,
allspice and Szechuan pepper.

Heat a tablespoon of oil in a frying pan over medium-high
heat. Add the onion, garlic, chilli and red pepper and sweat for
5 minutes, until the onion is softened. Add the fried tofu and toss
to mix. Transfer the mixture to a large bowl. Stir in the seasoning.

Make the dipping sauce. Combine all the ingredients in a small
bowl and mix well.

Serve the tofu with the dipping sauce or on a bed of rice with
the dipping sauce poured on top.

TOFU STIR-FRY WITH GREENS

SERVES 2

300g (10½oz) udon noodles
vegetable oil, for frying
280g (10oz) firm tofu, cubed
1 red onion, thinly sliced
5 garlic cloves, thinly sliced
1 teaspoon finely chopped
  fresh root ginger
1–2 green chillies, sliced
1 small carrot, in ribbons
1 small courgette, in ribbons
½ green pepper, cored
  and cut into strips
100g (3½oz) rainbow
  chard, thinly sliced
100g (3½oz) sugar snap peas
200ml (7fl oz)
  vegetable stock
1 teaspoon cornflour

For the seasoning sauce
2 tablespoons soy sauce
1 tablespoon maple syrup
1 tablespoon toasted
  sesame oil

Stir-fries are ideal for quick, simple and flavourful meals. The cooking needs to be quick so whenever I make a stir-fry, I organize myself first, chopping and preparing everything in bowls (this is called my mise-en-place) so the cooking is smooth and efficient.

Make the seasoning sauce by mixing together all the ingredients.

Cook the noodles according to packet instructions.

Heat 3 tablespoons of oil in a wok or large frying pan over medium-high heat. Add the tofu and onion and fry for 3 minutes. Add the garlic and ginger and sauté for another 1–2 minutes. Add the chillies, carrot, courgette, green pepper, chard and sugar snap peas. Pour in the vegetable stock and toss for 2 minutes. Add the seasoning sauce and mix well.

In a small bowl, combine the cornflour with 1 teaspoon of water. Add to the wok and simmer, until the sauce has thickened. Stir in the noodles and cook until warmed through. Serve immediately.

Recipe pictured on page 93

★ PREP 5 MINUTES ★

HIGH-PROTEIN TOFU SHAKE

SERVES 1

50g (1¾oz) soy pulp (see
  page 92)
½ banana
2 tablespoons frozen berries
1 tablespoon date syrup
1 tablespoon sunflower seeds
1 tablespoon chia seeds
300ml (10fl oz) plant-
  based milk

This is perfect for post-gym (swim, cycle or run) recovery.

Blitz all the ingredients in a blender until smooth. Serve in a glass, decorated with the extra sunflower and chia seeds, if you like.

VEGAN SAUSAGE and ORZO CASSEROLE

SERVES 4

8 vegan sausages
virgin olive oil, for frying
3 shallots, finely chopped
3 celery sticks, chopped
4–5 garlic cloves, finely chopped
300g (10½oz) mushrooms, trimmed and chopped
100ml (3½fl oz) white wine
1 tablespoon tomato purée
400g (14oz) tomatoes, chopped
400g (14oz) can chopped tomatoes
dash of vegan Worcestershire sauce
dash of maple syrup
500ml (18fl oz) vegetable stock
handful of baby spinach
5 sprigs of thyme, plus extra to garnish
2 bay leaves
130g (4¾oz) orzo
salt and pepper

While I was rowing across the Atlantic back in 2021, we would pack dehydrated meals in thick sealable foil bags. When we needed fuel, we'd rehydrate them in boiling water. My favourite meal on the boat was, by far, an orzo Bolognese. Orzo pasta is so versatile – I use it to replace rice and add it to stews such as this comforting vegan sausage casserole. It's a lovely winter warmer all in one pan!

Cook the vegan sausages according to packet instructions. Chop into bite-sized pieces and set aside.

Heat 2 tablespoons of oil in a casserole over medium-high heat. Add the shallots and celery and sweat for 5 minutes, until softened. Add the garlic, mushrooms and white wine and sauté for another 5 minutes. Stir in the tomato purée and cook for another 5 minutes. Add the fresh and canned tomatoes and simmer for 10 minutes.

Preheat the oven to 180°C (350°F), Gas Mark 4.

Stir in the vegan sausages to the pan. Add the vegan Worcestershire sauce and maple syrup. Pour in the stock, then season with salt and pepper.

Add the spinach and cook for a minute, until wilted. Add the thyme, bay leaves and orzo and mix well.

Cover and bake for 35 minutes, until the orzo is cooked through.

Discard the woody thyme stems and bay leaves, then garnish with the extra thyme sprigs and serve.

VEGAN 'CHICKEN' and SWEETCORN PIE

SERVES 4

50g (1¾oz) Vegan Butter
(see page 36)
450g (1lb) leeks, trimmed,
cleaned and cut into
1-cm (½-inch) slices
3 garlic cloves, finely chopped
2 tablespoons chopped chives
1 tablespoon thyme leaves
a grating of nutmeg
2 tablespoons plain flour,
plus extra for dusting
240g (8½oz) vegan chicken
150g (5½oz) frozen sweetcorn
1 teaspoon Dijon mustard
400ml (14fl oz) plant-based milk
500g (1lb 2oz) block of vegan
puff pastry, defrosted if frozen
salt and pepper

Who doesn't like a pie? Here, a lovely puff pastry is packed with a comforting and savoury filling of vegan chicken and sweet pops of sweetcorn.

Heat the vegan butter in a frying pan over medium heat. Add the leeks and sweat for 5 minutes. Add the garlic and sweat for another 3 minutes. Stir in the chives, thyme and nutmeg. Sprinkle in the flour, then stir in the vegan chicken and corn. The mixture will turn gloopy but continue to stir until it's mixed in. Stir in the mustard.

Slowly pour in the plant-based milk and stir until the sauce is smooth. Transfer the mixture to a 25-cm (10-inch) ovenproof dish.

Preheat the oven to 190°C (375°F), Gas Mark 5.

Roll out the pastry on a lightly floured surface. Cut a circle about 2cm (¾ inch) larger than your ovenproof dish. Cut the remaining pastry scraps into shapes of your choice to decorate the pie. Place the trimmed pastry over the dish, gently tucking in the edges. Using a fork, poke a few steam holes into the centre of the pastry. Decorate the top of the pie with the pastry cut-outs. Bake for 25 minutes, until the pastry is a deep golden brown and cooked through. If needed, bake for another 5 minutes.

Remove the pie from the oven, get a big spoon and serve it up.

THE DANCING FALAFEL BOWL

SERVES 2

For the falafel
3 garlic cloves
½ red onion, roughly chopped
400g (14oz) can chickpeas,
    drained and rinsed (reserve
    the liquid to use as aquafaba
    in other recipes)
25g (1oz) coriander
2 tablespoons chickpea flour
1 teaspoon ground coriander
1 teaspoon ground cumin
1 tablespoon olive oil
½ teaspoon harissa paste
zest of 1 lemon
sunflower oil, for deep-frying
salt and pepper

For the bowl
100g (3½oz) buckwheat
50g (1¾oz) edamame beans
1 avocado
½ cucumber, thinly sliced
60g (2¼oz) rocket
4 tablespoons sunflower seeds
handful of cherry
    tomatoes, halved
handful of shredded red cabbage
Maple-Mustard Dressing
    (see page 141)

You can't beat a falafel. When added to a delicious bowl of buckwheat, salad and a tasty sauce, it packs an ambitious protein punch and makes you want to get dancing.

Make the falafel. Combine all the ingredients, except the sunflower oil, in a food processor. Blitz until the texture is fine and grainy. (You want to be able to bind them into balls without them falling apart.) Shape the mixture into 8 large, or 12 small, balls. Press firmly into shape.

Heat the sunflower oil in a deep fryer or deep saucepan to 180°C (350°F), or until a cube of bread browns in 30 seconds. (Alternatively, bake the falafel in a preheated 200°C (400°F), Gas Mark 6 for 20–25 minutes.) Working in batches, carefully lower the falafel into the hot oil and deep-fry for 3–4 minutes, until golden. Transfer the cooked falafel to a plate lined with kitchen paper to drain. Repeat with the remaining falafel.

Make the filling. Cook the buckwheat according to packet instructions. It should be 500ml (18fl oz) of water to 100g (3½oz) of buckwheat. Drain.

If the edamame beans are frozen, then pour some boiling water over them to defrost. Drain.

Put the buckwheat into individual bowls. Now, let your imagination run wild and top them up with the remaining ingredients as you like. Drizzle with dressing and feast!

SEITAN TACOS WITH BUTTER BEAN HUMMUS

SERVES 2

Yeehaw, do I have a smoky, chilli-packed recipe in store for you! These bad boy tacos ain't gonna let you down. Seitan – which, funnily enough, sounds like 'satan' – is a meat substitute and not the devil himself! Full of protein goodness, it dates back 1,500 years to ancient China, where it was made by vegetarian Buddhist monks. My first cookbook features a recipe for chorizo seitan sausage, which would be great for this recipe. Failing that, you can buy seitan at the supermarket.

For the butter bean hummus
120g (4¼oz) butter beans
1 garlic clove
50ml (2fl oz) water
1½ tablespoons tahini
½ teaspoon lemon juice
salt and white pepper

For the seasoning
½ teaspoon dried oregano
1 teaspoon chilli powder,
   or to taste
1 teaspoon smoked
   paprika
1 teaspoon ground cumin

For the seitan tacos
virgin olive oil, for frying
1 onion, finely chopped
3 garlic cloves,
   finely chopped
1 red chilli,
   finely chopped
200g (7oz) seitan,
   chopped into mince
2 tablespoons water
1 tablespoon liquid smoke
6 soft tortillas
100g (3½oz) shredded
   vegan mozzarella
   (optional)
2 tomatoes,
   finely chopped
1 avocado, chopped
10g (¼oz) coriander,
   roughly chopped

Make the butter bean hummus. In a food processor, combine all the ingredients and blitz for 3 minutes, until smooth and velvety. Adjust the seasoning to taste.

Make the seasoning. In a small bowl, combine all the ingredients and mix well.

Make the seitan tacos. Heat 2 tablespoons of oil in a frying pan over medium heat. Add the onion and sweat for 7 minutes, until softened and slightly browned. Add the garlic and chilli and cook for another 2 minutes. Stir in the seitan and fry for 3 minutes.

Stir in the seasoning. Add the measured water and liquid smoke to prevent the mixture from drying out and burning the spices. If needed, add a little more water. Cook for 5 minutes.

Heat a frying pan over medium heat. Add a tortilla and heat for a few seconds on each side, until warmed up and softened. Transfer to a plate, then repeat with the remaining tortillas.

Slather the butter bean hummus onto your tortillas, then top with the seitan mixture. Add the vegan mozzarella, if using, tomatoes, avocado and coriander and fold up your taco.

Serve. Chef's kiss.

GUEST CHEF: LAURA GRAHAM FROM TIDY KITCHEN
SPICY PROTEIN BOWLS
SERVES 2

For the spice rub
2 teaspoons paprika
1 teaspoon ground cumin
1 teaspoon chipotle chilli flakes
pinch of salt
drizzle of olive oil

For the bowl
1 sweet potato, cut into
    bite-sized cubes
1 red pepper, cored,
    deseeded and sliced
½ red onion, chopped
80g (2¾oz) cooked chickpeas
400g (14oz) can black beans,
    drained and rinsed
4 tablespoons pecan nuts
½ tablespoon maple syrup

For the slaw
1 carrot, grated
¼ red cabbage, thinly sliced
¼ white cabbage, thinly sliced
handful of coriander, stems finely
    chopped, leaves reserved
2 tablespoons extra virgin
    olive oil
1 tablespoon lime juice

For the toppings
½ avocado, mashed
1 tablespoon chia seeds
8 cherry tomatoes, chopped
Sriracha (optional)
reserved coriander leaves from
    the slaw, roughly chopped
spring onions, finely sliced
    (optional)

Laura Graham and her family have been providing support and guidance on- and off-camera, since the very first series of Dirty Vegan. *It's been amazing working with her, shooting the series and doing food events together. Thank you, Laura – you are a legend. #BookWine. Laura is also the brains behind Tidy Kitchen, an online food service offering tasty plant-based dishes 'with a conscience' and I had to include a recipe. This protein-packed bowl keeps you nourished, fuelled and satisfied. Pumped with nutrient-rich chia seeds, pulses and legumes, this colourful, healthy and balanced meal-in-a-bowl will leave you satiated and full of beans (literally).*

Make the spice rub. Combine all the ingredients in a small bowl and mix well.

Preheat the oven to 200°C (400°F), Gas Mark 6.

To make the spicy protein bowls, combine the sweet potato, red pepper, onion and chickpeas on a baking sheet. Add the spice rub, reserving 1 teaspoon for the black beans. Toss to evenly coat, then roast for 25 minutes, or until a knife can easily pierce the sweet potatoes without resistance.

Meanwhile, in a small saucepan, combine the black beans and the reserved teaspoon of spice rub. Heat over medium heat until warmed through. Set aside.

Line another baking sheet with baking parchment. Add the pecans and maple syrup and roast for 5 minutes. Keep an eye on this as the pecans can burn quickly.

Make the slaw. In a bowl, combine all the ingredients and toss. Set aside.

Time to assemble. Divide the warm beans between 2 bowls. Add the roasted vegetables and a spoonful of slaw. Top with sweet crunchy pecans, avocado, chia seeds and cherry tomatoes. Drizzle with Sriracha and sprinkle with coriander and spring onions, if using.

Serve.

MARINATED TEMPEH and ROAST SPROUTS

SERVES 2

For the marinated tempeh
2 garlic cloves, crushed
4 tablespoons balsamic vinegar
1 tablespoon toasted sesame oil
1 tablespoon maple syrup
200g (7oz) tempeh, cut into
    bite-sized pieces
salt and pepper

For the Brussels sprouts
400g (14oz) Brussels sprouts,
    trimmed and halved
2 tablespoons olive oil
2 tablespoons balsamic vinegar
80g (2¾oz) sunflower seeds
salt and pepper

For the spicy aioli
6 tablespoons vegan mayonnaise
2 garlic cloves, grated
1 tablespoon Sriracha

I look forward to cooking Brussels sprouts every year, in late autumn when they're in season. They're so good for you and full of flavour, especially when roasted. Tempeh, on the other hand, is a different story. I've never been a fan, but it's been on my radar recently and I enjoy it here in this dish. If you're looking for a protein-pumped snack that is tasty, hearty, and perfect for slow-release energy, this, my friend, is the dish for you.

Make the marinated tempeh. Combine all the ingredients, except for the tempeh in a freezer bag. Season with salt and pepper and mix well. Add the tempeh and mix to coat. Seal the bag, removing as much of the air as possible. Leave in the fridge to marinate for at least 30 minutes but preferably overnight.

Make the Brussels sprouts. Preheat the oven to 200°C (400°F), Gas Mark 6.

Combine the sprouts and olive oil in a bowl. Season with salt and pepper. Toss to coat.

Add the tempeh and mix. Spread out the mixture onto a baking sheet. Roast for 15 minutes. Give it a good stir, then drizzle with the balsamic vinegar. Scatter with sunflower seeds. Bake for another 15 minutes.

Meanwhile, make the spicy aioli. Combine all the ingredients in a small bowl.

Put the tempeh and sprouts into a bowl and serve with spicy aioli. Get ready for dipping time.

RED LENTIL SOUP
SERVES 6

For the soup
2 red peppers, cored,
  deseeded and left whole
2–3 tomatoes, halved
virgin olive oil, for drizzling
  and frying
1 onion, chopped
1 carrot, cut into 1-cm
  (½-inch) cubes
4 garlic cloves, finely chopped
200g (7oz) split red
  lentils, rinsed
2 tablespoons nutritional yeast
1 teaspoon ground cumin
1 teaspoon smoked paprika
1 litre (1¾ pints) vegetable stock
3 sprigs of oregano
1 teaspoon coconut sugar
  or brown sugar
250ml (9fl oz) coconut milk
1 teaspoon balsamic vinegar
salt and pepper

To garnish
plant-based cream, for drizzling
chilli flakes, for sprinkling
hemp seeds, for sprinkling

When I was kid, I thought hippies were the only people who ate lentils. I eventually realized I couldn't be further away from the truth. Lentils are so incredibly versatile with countless ways to prepare them. Here, I've simmered split red lentils with delicious veg and mega seasoning for a comforting bowl of nourishment.

Make the soup. Preheat the oven to 200°C (400°F), Gas Mark 6.

Place the peppers and tomatoes on a baking sheet. Drizzle with olive oil, then season generously with salt and pepper. Roast for 25 minutes.

Meanwhile, heat 2 tablespoons of oil in a frying pan over medium-high heat. Add the onion, carrot and garlic and sweat for 7 minutes, until softened.

Add the lentils, nutritional yeast, cumin and smoked paprika. Pour in the stock and mix well. Bring to a boil.

Tie the sprigs of oregano together with kitchen string to make a bouquet garni. Add this to the soup. Reduce the heat to medium-low and simmer for 15 minutes. Discard the oregano and tip the roasted peppers and tomatoes into the soup pan.

Using a hand blender, blitz the soup until smooth. (Alternatively, use a standard blender.) Heat up the soup over medium heat. Add the sugar, then stir in the coconut milk and balsamic. Adjust the seasoning to taste.

Finish with a swirl of plant-based cream (oooh, so posh!), then sprinkle with chilli flakes and hemp seeds. Tuck in.

SILKEN TOFU and SHIITAKE RAMEN

SERVES 4

30g (1oz) dried porcini
    mushrooms
300ml (10fl oz) boiling water
virgin olive oil, for frying
1 onion, finely chopped
3 garlic cloves, finely chopped
2.5-cm (1-inch) piece of
    fresh root ginger
125g (4½oz) shiitake
    mushrooms, sliced
1 litre (1¾ pints) hot
    vegetable stock
1 nori sheet, cut into strips
    (optional)
2 tablespoons red or white
    miso paste
350g (12oz) silken tofu, cut
    into 2-cm (¾-inch) cubes
400g (14oz) ramen noodles,
    to serve

To garnish
bean sprouts
radishes, finely chopped
spring onions, thinly sliced

Japan is one of my favourite countries to visit. Seriously, the cities are so clean, the people are so lovely, the culture is so respectful and their food is otherworldly. On my last visit, before I became vegan, I had ramen all the time. I wanted to enjoy all the elements of ramen as a vegan. Here is my Welsh take on savoury vegan soup noodles, perfect for fuelling the body on a chilly day.

Put the dried porcini mushrooms in a bowl and add the measured water. Set aside to rehydrate.

Meanwhile, heat 1 tablespoon of oil in a frying pan over medium-high heat. Add the onion and sweat for 7 minutes, until translucent. Add the garlic and ginger and sauté for another minute. Add the shiitakes and sauté for 2 minutes.

Drain the porcini, reserving the soaking liquid (it is full of umami flavour and will help add depth to your sauce.) Squeeze out all the excess water from the porcini, then finely chop them and add to the pan of veg with the vegetable stock and nori, if using. Pour in the soaking liquid, taking care to leave out any bits of grit at the bottom. You definitely do not want that in your stock. Reduce the heat to medium-low and simmer for 25 minutes.

Stir in the miso and cook for 5 minutes. Carefully add the silken tofu. It's delicate so it's okay if some of it breaks.

Cook your ramen noodles according to packet instructions.

Let's get ready to serve. Divide the noodles between 4 bowls and pour over the soup. Garnish with bean sprouts, radish and spring onions and tuck in.

PEANUT BUTTER PANCAKES WITH A SWEET NUT DRIZZLE

MAKES ABOUT 14

For the pancakes
200g (7oz) porridge oats
150g (5½oz) pumpkin seeds
2 bananas, roughly chopped
1 teaspoon baking powder
500ml (18fl oz) plant-based milk
virgin olive oil, for frying

For the nut drizzle
200ml (7fl oz) oat or soy cream
4 tablespoons almond or
    peanut butter
2 tablespoons maple syrup

For the toppings
1 banana, chopped
peanuts, cashew nuts
    or almonds, crushed
sunflower seeds

My goal was to boost the protein content of these pancakes, so I added pumpkin seeds. They are one of the best sources of complete protein, boasting nine essential amino acids required by your body. And that sweet peanut sauce? It's ridiculously good.

Make the pancakes. Combine the oats and pumpkin seeds in a food processor and blitz to a fine powder. Add the bananas, baking powder and milk and mix for 3 minutes, or until smooth.

Heat 1 teaspoon of oil in a nonstick frying pan over medium heat. Ladle the batter into the pan and fry for 1 minute on each side, or until cooked through. Transfer the pancake to a plate, then repeat until you've used up all the batter.

Make the nut drizzle. In a bowl, combine all the ingredients and mix well.

Stack your pancakes, then drizzle with ample sauce so it oozes down the sides. Top with chopped banana, crushed nuts and sunflower seeds. It's now ready to serve!

HIGH-PROTEIN GRANOLA

SERVES 7~8

200g (7oz) porridge oats
100g (3½oz) sunflower seeds
100g (3½oz) pistachio nuts
100g (3½oz) vegan
    protein powder
1 tablespoon chia seeds
1 tablespoon ground cinnamon
1 tablespoon ground nutmeg
1 tablespoon ground ginger
5 tablespoons maple syrup
5 tablespoons Vegan Butter
    (see page 36)
5 tablespoons coconut oil
2 tablespoons vanilla bean paste
100g (3½oz) vegan
    chocolate chips
70g (2½oz) cranberries
70g (2½oz) raisins

You will never buy shop-bought granola again. Why? Because making your own is far more fun and tastier. Consider doubling or tripling this recipe. This way, when you need to dash out the door, there's no need to skip breakfast 'cuz this power granola will be ready and waiting for you. You can easily have it for a snack or sprinkled over smoothies, too. Just be sure to store it in an airtight container.

Preheat the oven to 170°C (340°F), Gas Mark 3½.

In a large bowl, combine the oats, sunflower seeds, pistachios, protein powder, chia seeds and spices. Mix well.

In a small saucepan, combine the maple syrup, vegan butter, coconut oil and vanilla and mix well. Heat over medium heat. Drizzle this into the bowl of the oat mixture and mix well.

Spread out the mixture on a baking sheet. Bake for 10 minutes. Stir, then bake for another 10 minutes. Set aside to cool.

Add the vegan chocolate chips, cranberries and raisins.

Store it in an airtight container for up to 1 month.

COCONUT SMOOTHIE BOWL

SERVES 2

3 bananas, peeled and frozen
1 teaspoon vanilla bean paste
3 tablespoons vanilla
vegan protein powder
150ml (5fl oz) canned
coconut milk

For the salted caramel
20g (¾oz) Vegan Butter
(see page 36)
2 tablespoons maple syrup
1 tablespoon plant-based
cream (I used oat)
½ teaspoon vanilla bean paste
pinch of sea salt

For the toppings (optional)
bananas
berries
black sesame seeds
cacao nibs
chia seeds
High-Protein Granola
(see page 113)
nut butters
nuts
coconut flakes

My fiancée Ciara and I once spent an amazing three weeks in Bali. Sure, we wanted a relaxing tropical holiday, but we were also drawn to the huge choice of vegan eateries. Plant-based restaurants, cafés and bars were everywhere. On our first morning, I ordered a smoothie bowl for breakfast – and wow. It was a complete revelation, and I've been hooked on them since. When I returned home, I bought a load of coconut bowls and created my own smoothie bowls. What I love most about them is the flexibility to make it as you like. Top it with granola, fruit, nuts, seeds, anything you fancy... you really can't go wrong.

Cut up the frozen bananas into chunks. In a food processor, combine the frozen banana chunks and vanilla and blitz until the bananas begin to breakdown. Add the protein powder and coconut milk and blitz until smooth.

Make the salted caramel. Combine all the ingredients in a small pan and bring to a boil. Boil for 10 minutes, until caramel-like in colour and consistency. Set aside to cool.

Transfer the banana smoothie into a coconut bowl or a regular bowl. Top with your favourite toppings, drizzle with the salted caramel and enjoy!

CHAPTER
5

SUMMER
SMASHERS

I absolutely love the summer, it puts a huge smile on my face. On the flip side, I despise the winter, but as soon as summer starts, all its lovely fresh produce hits our supermarkets and we can start cooking some nice light, tasty and deliciously fresh summery recipes. These next few pages have some beauties in them. Enjoy!

PAPAYA SALAD

For the salad
100g (3½oz) edamame beans
2 carrots, sliced into thin strips
1 red pepper, cored, deseeded
    and sliced into thin strips
1 green papaya or underripe
    mango, shredded
½ Chinese leaf lettuce,
    sliced into thin strips
½ white cabbage,
    sliced into thin strips
handful of mint,
    roughly chopped
handful of Thai basil,
    roughly chopped
handful of coriander,
    roughly chopped
50g (1¾oz) crushed peanuts

For the sauce
2 garlic cloves
2 red chillies, or to taste
juice of 1 lime
1 teaspoon palm sugar
1 teaspoon tamarind paste
    or 1 tablespoon lime juice
1 teaspoon vegan fish sauce
3 tablespoons toasted sesame oil

Whenever I visit Bangkok, choosing the right stall to go to is always a challenge. The food is absolutely bang-on, and we are always spoilt for choice. A refreshing spicy papaya salad to accompany your meal is a classic. I've created something similar so I can bring the flavours and memories of Thailand back home. I hope you all like this one as much as I do!

Make the salad. If the edamame beans are frozen, then pour some boiling water over them to defrost. Drain.

In a medium bowl, combine all the ingredients and toss together well.

Make the sauce. In a food processor, combine all the ingredients and pulse until smooth (or I tend to use a pestle and mortar).

Stir three-quarters of the sauce into the salad and mix to coat the salad. Adjust to taste with more sauce.

Eat straight away.

ROAST SPICED CHICKPEAS and QUINOA SALAD

SERVES 2

Chickpeas... my little vegan friends. They're essential in making creamy hummus, stews, curries and the salad prepared here. They are spiced and roasted to perfection to give some textural crunch to this colourful salad. Plus, a 164g (5¾oz) serving packs 14.5g (½oz) of protein.

For the roasted chickpeas
400g (14oz) can chickpeas, drained and rinsed (reserve the liquid to use as aquafaba in other recipes)
2 tablespoons olive oil
2 teaspoons smoked paprika
2 teaspoons ground cumin
1 teaspoon onion powder
1 teaspoon garlic powder
salt and pepper

For the salad
100g (3½oz) quinoa
80g (2¾oz) rocket
½ red onion, thin sliced
¼ cucumber, thinly sliced
150g (5½oz) cherry tomatoes, halved
80g (2¾oz) black or Kalamata olives, pitted and sliced
130g (4¾oz) vegan feta, cubed

For the vinaigrette
2 garlic cloves, crushed
50g (1¾oz) unsweetened coconut yogurt
2 tablespoons white wine vinegar
1 teaspoon tahini
1 teaspoon maple syrup
salt and pepper

Make the roasted chickpeas. Preheat the oven to 200°C (400°F), Gas Mark 6.

Tip the chickpeas onto a clean tea towel and pat them dry as much as you can. Place on a baking sheet and drizzle with the olive oil. Shuffle the chickpeas until they are coated. Sprinkle with the paprika, cumin, onion powder and garlic powder. Season with salt and pepper and shuffle again to ensure the chickpea are well-coated. Roast for 20–25 minutes.

Meanwhile, make the salad. Bring a small saucepan of water to a boil. Add the quinoa and cook for 20 minutes, until tender and cooked. Drain.

Remove the chickpeas from the oven and set aside to cool slightly.

Place the rocket on a nice serving platter. Build the salad with the remaining ingredients except the vegan feta.

Make the vinaigrette. Combine all the ingredients in a jar. Secure the lid and shake it. (If you don't have a jar, just mix them in a bowl.)

Sprinkle the quinoa, roasted chickpeas and feta on top. Drizzle with the vinaigrette. Serve.

ROAST CARROT and SMOKED TOFU SALAD

SERVES 4

For the almond dressing
1 garlic clove, crushed
½ lime
4 tablespoons almond butter
2 tablespoons balsamic vinegar
1 tablespoon maple syrup
1 teaspoon toasted sesame oil
salt and pepper

For the salad
400g (14oz) rainbow carrots,
    roughly chopped
3 tablespoons extra virgin
    olive oil
60g (2¼oz) wholemeal couscous
75ml (2½fl oz) boiling water
100g (3½oz) kale, chopped
200g (7oz) smoked tofu (I used
    a version with almonds and
    sesame seeds), chopped
3 spring onions, chopped
½ pomegranate, halved
salt and pepper

It is my mission to prove that vegan food doesn't have to be boring. This salad is a perfect example: it's full of colour and flavour; plus, the off-the-charts almond dressing has a sweet and sour tang that cuts through the carrots and smoked tofu. Then pops of pomegranate add bursts of sweetness. Bland? This is anything but.

Preheat the oven to 200°C (400°F), Gas Mark 6.

Make the dressing. Combine all the ingredients in a jar. Secure the lid and shake together (or mix in a bowl).

Make the salad. Put the carrots on a baking sheet. Drizzle with 2 tablespoons of olive oil, then season with salt and pepper. Shake to coat. Roast for 20 minutes, or until tender. Set aside to cool.

Put your couscous in a heatproof bowl and cover with the measured water. Cover and set aside for 5 minutes, or until the couscous has absorbed the water. Using a fork, loosen up the couscous and set aside to cool.

Massage the kale with the remaining tablespoon of olive oil. Add a pinch of salt. Add 2cm (¾ inch) boiling water to a large saucepan. Place the kale in a steamer basket over the saucepan, then cover. Steam for 1–2 minutes, until softened slightly. Set aside to cool.

In a medium bowl, combine the carrots, couscous, kale and tofu. Toss to mix. Sprinkle with the spring onions and pomegranate seeds. Pour your dressing evenly over the salad, then grab a big fat spoon and dig in.

THREE-BEAN SALAD IN A JAR

MAKES 2

For the salad
1 yellow pepper, cored,
   deseeded and finely chopped
1 avocado, diced
½ cucumber, finely chopped
½ red onion, finely chopped
100g (3½oz) cherry tomatoes,
   halved or quartered
2 tablespoons lime juice
400g (14oz) can cannellini
   beans, drained and rinsed
400g (14oz) can red kidney
   beans, drained and rinsed
100g (3½oz) edamame beans,
   defrosted if frozen
1 carrot, grated
½ red cabbage, shredded
2–3 romaine or iceberg
   lettuce, chopped
handful of crushed peanuts,
   for sprinkling
salt and pepper

For the vinaigrette
2 tablespoons balsamic vinegar
2 tablespoons olive oil
2 teaspoons Dijon mustard
1 teaspoon maple syrup
salt and pepper

Lunch in a jar. This recipe makes enough for at least two meals: prep it on a Sunday, then have them ready for your Monday and Tuesdays workdays. Be sure to layer the jars properly – the wet ingredients should be at the bottom while the dry ones sit at the top so they don't go soggy. I also keep the vinaigrette separate in a small jar. Come lunchtime, pour the vinaigrette on top of the salad and enjoy this healthy lunch break. Happy days.

Make the salad. In a bowl, combine the pepper, avocado, cucumber, red onion and cherry tomatoes. Season with salt and pepper, then drizzle in the lime juice and mix well.

Combine the beans and edamame in a bowl and mix.

Now it's time to fill your jars. Layer 2 large jars with the tomato salad. In this order, add the carrot, red cabbage and bean mixture. Fill with the chopped lettuce and sprinkle with crushed peanuts. Cover with the lids, then put them in the fridge.

Make the vinaigrette. Combine all the ingredients in a small jar. Secure the lid and shake it.

When ready to serve, open your big salad jar, pour in the vinaigrette and give it a good mix. The salad jars last a good 3 days in the fridge.

QUICHE LORRAINE

SERVES 4

For the pastry base
plain flour, for dusting
500g (1lb 2oz) pack of vegan
    ready-made shortcrust pastry

For the vegan crème fraîche
125g (4½oz) cashew nuts,
    soaked overnight (see Note)
200ml (7fl oz) plant-based
    milk, plus extra if needed
1 tablespoon lemon juice

For the tofu cream
300g (10½oz) firm tofu,
    crumbled
4 tablespoons nutritional yeast
100ml (3½fl oz) plant-based milk
salt and pepper

For the quiche
virgin olive oil, for frying
½ red onion, thinly sliced
2 garlic cloves, finely chopped
120g (4¼oz) vegan lardons
150g (5½oz) broccoli florets
150g (5½oz) vegan cheese
1 large beefsteak tomato, sliced
chives (optional), to serve

NOTE
If you don't have the time to
soak your cashew nuts overnight,
simply put them into a bowl with
boiling water for 3 hours to soak.

*When I was a kid, we'd have quiche Lorraine with new
potatoes and baked beans on weekly rotation, so preparing
this dish brought back so many happy memories of my
family sitting around the table and tucking into this simple
meal. (Yes, that's how we used to eat back then.) I took over
my parents' kitchen when I created it. This way, they could
eat it and I could keep a slice for myself. Plus, the experience
reminded Mam of when she cooked it for us many years
ago. I love how food has the power to take you back many
years. You'll need to soak the cashews overnight, so plan
a day ahead.*

Make the pastry base. Preheat the oven to 190°C (375°F),
Gas Mark 5.

Roll out the pastry on a lightly floured surface, about 5cm
(2 inches) wider than the circumference of your flan tin.
(I used a 22-cm/8½-inch fluted flan tin.) Carefully pick up
your pastry so it doesn't break and line your tin with it.
Trim off any excess pastry.

To blind bake the pastry base, line it with baking paper
and fill with baking beans (or dried beans). Blind bake for
15 minutes, then remove the paper and beans. Return it
to the oven and bake, uncovered, for another 5 minutes.
Set aside to cool. Leave the oven on.

Meanwhile, prepare the vegan crème fraîche. Drain the cashews, then put them in a blender. Pour in enough plant-based milk to cover the cashews by 2.5cm (1 inch). (Avoid using too much milk; otherwise, the sauce will be runny.) Add the lemon juice and salt and blitz until smooth and creamy. Transfer the mixture to a big bowl.

Make the tofu cream. In a food processor, combine all the ingredients and blitz until smooth. Add to the vegan crème fraîche and mix well.

Make the quiche. Heat 1 tablespoon of oil in a frying pan over medium heat. Add the onion and garlic and sweat for 5 minutes. Add the vegan lardons and sauté for another 5 minutes. Pour this into the vegan crème fraîche. Add the broccoli florets and 120g (4¼oz) of vegan cheese. Stir to combine.

Pour the filling into the cooked pastry case. Sprinkle with the remaining 20g (¾oz) of vegan cheese. Top with sliced tomato. Bake for 30–35 minutes, until deep golden brown.

Let cool, then serve.

CARAMELIZED BALSAMIC RED ONION & SOFT CHEESE PUFF TARTS

SERVES 4

virgin olive oil, for frying
2 red onions, halved and
    thinly sliced
2 teaspoon dark brown sugar
2 teaspoon balsamic vinegar
500g (1lb 2oz) vegan puff
    pastry, defrosted if frozen
plain flour, for dusting
150g (5½oz) vegan cream cheese
9 cherry tomatoes, halved
3 sprigs of thyme
plant-based milk or Vegan Butter
    (see page 36), for brushing

To garnish
balsamic glaze, for drizzling
chopped cashew nuts, toasted
rocket

Puff pastry with delicious caramelized onions and soft cheese. What's not to like?

Heat 2–3 tablespoons of olive oil in a frying pan over medium-low heat. Add the onions and sweat for 15 minutes, until softened. Add the sugar and balsamic and cook for another 10 minutes, the onions are sticky.

Roll out the pastry on a lightly floured surface to a thickness of 5mm (¼ inch). Using a knife, drag a line around the pastry, designate a 2-cm (¾-inch) border around the pastry. This will give a nice crust when baked. Do not cut through the pastry!

Using a fork, pierce all over within this border.

Whip up your vegan cheese until light and fluffy. Spread the cream cheese within the indented border. Scatter the balsamic onions on top. Add the cherry tomatoes and thyme sprigs.

Preheat the oven to 200°C (400°F), Gas Mark 6. Brush the borders of the pastry with the plant-based milk (or vegan butter). Bake for 30 minutes, until the tart is cooked through.

Drizzle the tart with balsamic glaze, sprinkle with cashews and top with rocket.

Slice and serve.

VEGAN 'TUNA' LETTUCE WRAPS

SERVES 4–8

4 small gherkins, finely chopped
1 celery stick, finely chopped
½ red onion, finely chopped
400g (14oz) can chickpeas,
    drained and rinsed (reserve
    the liquid to use as aquafaba
    in other recipes)
2 teaspoons capers, drained
1 nori sheet, scrunched,
    or a handful of seaweed thins
3 tablespoons vegan mayo
2 teaspoons tahini
1 teaspoon wholegrain mustard
½ teaspoon garlic powder
dash of sherry vinegar
zest and juice of ½ lemon
1–2 heads of romaine lettuce,
    leaves separated
salt and pepper
lemon wedges, to serve

I had these at a party many years ago and I wanted to create them. This easy dish is designed for large parties. Remember: This is a sharing platter for you and your mates, not for you to eat alone and stuff your face! Store-bought vegan mayo is widely available, but I also have a recipe for it in my first book Dirty Vegan.

In a large bowl, combine the gherkins, celery, red onion, chickpeas, capers and nori. Using a potato masher, mash it all together.

In a small bowl, combine the vegan mayo, tahini, mustard, garlic powder, vinegar and lemon zest and juice. Mix well, then add to the bowl of veg. Toss well, then season to taste with salt and pepper.

Grab good-looking pieces of romaine lettuce and fill with the vegan 'tuna'. Serve with lemon wedges on the side to squeeze over and eat away. The refreshing mouthfuls are brilliant. Enjoy!

PREP 15 MINUTES ★ COOK 40–45 MINUTES

CANARIAN POTATOES WITH MOJO SAUCE

·SERVES 4·

1 garlic bulb
2 red peppers, cored
  and deseeded
3 tablespoons olive oil
750g (1lb 10oz) small
  waxy potatoes (Jersey
  Royals, Charlottes
  or fingerlings)
1–2 red chillies, to taste
1 slice of bread, de-crusted
2 teaspoons sea salt
2 tablespoons red wine
  vinegar (see Note)

NOTE
Depending on what red wine
was used, some vinegars are
not vegan. Check the bottle
or with the manufacturer.

Spain is my destination in life: I want to live there and have a nice house with a lovely roof garden and outdoor kitchen, somewhere quiet with a view of the sea. My fiancée and I are currently looking at houses so hopefully we can get a place and enjoy the Spanish lifestyle, the fantastic food and wine soon. I just love this popular Canarian dish. Years ago, when the islands lacked fresh water, these potatoes were cooked in sea water, giving them a distinct saltiness. And the delicious sauce bursts with flavour. We recently had a holiday in Gran Canaria, and it happened to be the first thing I ordered as soon as we hit our first restaurant.

Preheat the oven to 200°C (400°F), Gas Mark 6.

Slice a few millimetres off the top of the garlic bulb so you can just see a little flesh of the garlic cloves inside their papery skins. Place the garlic and peppers into the oven on a baking tray, drizzle with a tablespoon of olive oil and roast for 30 minutes. Set aside to cool.

Meanwhile, bring a saucepan of heavily salted water to a boil. Add the potatoes and boil for 10–15 minutes. (The time will depend on the size of the potatoes.) Drain, then set aside.

Put the peppers into a food processor, then squeeze in all the soft, juicy garlic cloves. Add the remaining ingredients (use 1 chilli if you prefer it milder) and blitz into a nice sauce. Drizzle the mojo sauce over your potatoes and serve.

SUMMER SMASHERS
134

SUMMER TIGER VEGGIE TRAY

SERVES 2

1 garlic bulb
400g (14oz) mixed tomatoes
200g (7oz) radishes
200g (7oz) green beans
4 tablespoons extra
   virgin olive oil
6 sprigs of rosemary
150g (5½oz) tiger bread,
   cut into thick chunks
salt and pepper

When the sun is out and the temperature is high, I want to eat veg at the height of the season – and this veggie tray sums of the flavours of summer perfectly. Tiger bread, a Dutch bread with a mottled crust, works best for this dish, but you can use any loaf. Use the bread as a sponge to soak up those incredible flavours.

Preheat the oven to 200°C (400°F), Gas Mark 6.

Wrap the garlic bulb in foil and roast in the oven for 20 minutes. Set aside to cool slightly.

When cool enough to handle, separate and peel the garlic cloves. Pop them onto a baking sheet, then add the tomatoes, radishes and green beans. Drizzle with olive oil, then season with salt and pepper. Toss to coat.

Spread the vegetables out on the baking sheet, then top with the sprigs of rosemary. Roast for 20 minutes.

Slot the tiger bread between the vegetables. Roast for 20 minutes, until the bread is toasted and has absorbed some of the veggie juices.

To serve, spread the roasted garlic onto the bread (it should spread like butter as it's so soft) and tuck in.

STUFFED PEPPERS
· SERVES 4 ·

100g (3½oz) brown rice
virgin olive oil, for frying
1 onion, finely chopped
1 celery stick, finely chopped
3 garlic cloves, finely chopped
1 tablespoon tomato purée
1 carrot, grated
400g (14oz) can chopped
  tomatoes
1 tablespoon dried basil
1 tablespoon dried oregano
4 red, orange or yellow
  peppers, cored, deseeded
  and tops reserved
salt and pepper
buttery potatoes and your
  choice of veg, to serve

Here's an eighties throwback! Sure, I know I'm showing my age, but my mother used to make us stuffed peppers for dinner when I was a kid. For a boost of veg, and to keep the price down, I've used grated carrot instead of plant mince. It works a treat.

Preheat the oven to 180°C (350°F), Gas Mark 4.

Cook your rice according to packet instructions.

Heat 2 tablespoons of oil in a frying pan over medium heat. Add the onion and celery and sweat for 7 minutes, until the onion is softened and translucent. Add the garlic and sauté for another 3 minutes.

Stir in the tomato purée. Add the carrot and cook for another 2 minutes.

Add the canned tomatoes, basil and oregano and simmer for 5 minutes. Add the cooked rice to the mixture and season generously with salt and pepper.

Stuff each pepper to the top with the filling. Gently place the lids on top. Place on a baking sheet and bake for 1 hour, until cooked through.

Now's the time to prepare your potatoes and choice of veg.

To serve, plate each pepper and serve with the potatoes and veg.

TOMATOES and TOFU SALAD

SERVES 2

150g (5½oz) firm tofu, sliced
4 ripe tomatoes, sliced
few basil leaves
capers, to garnish

For the vinaigrette
4 tablespoons extra virgin
   olive oil
1 tablespoon white wine vinegar
1 teaspoon Dijon mustard
1 teaspoon lemon juice
1 garlic clove, crushed
salt and pepper

I used to love tomatoes and buffalo mozzarella back in the day before I became vegan. These days, I just replace the mozzarella with tofu instead. The taste is totally different, but you get the idea. It makes a great starter before your main. Just be sure to buy fresh, high-quality tomatoes – they're an absolute must.

Arrange the tofu, tomatoes and basil on a plate, ensuring they overlap.

Make the vinaigrette. Combine all the ingredients in a jar. Secure the lid and shake it. (If you don't have a jar, just mix them in a bowl.)

Scatter capers on top, then drizzle vinaigrette over the entire salad.

Serve.

ZINGY VEGAN 'CHICKEN', SPINACH and ORZO SOUP

SERVES 4

virgin olive oil, for frying
1 onion, finely chopped
2 carrots, finely chopped
2 celery sticks, finely chopped
3 garlic cloves, finely chopped
100g (3½oz) orzo
1 litre (1¾ pints) vegetable stock
170g (2½oz) vegan chicken
1 tablespoon lemon juice
70g (2½oz) spinach
100g (3½oz) coconut milk
salt and pepper

This mega refreshing soup has a citrus kick, making it ideal for warm weather, al fresco meals. It is such a simple yet nutritious meal and hardly requires any time to make. I've got a thing for orzo these days, but you could easily replace it with another type of pasta.

Heat 2 tablespoons of oil in a frying pan over medium-high heat. Add the onion, carrots and celery and sweat for 7 minutes, until softened. Add the garlic and sauté for another 2–3 minutes.

Add the orzo and vegetable stock and bring to a boil. Reduce the heat to medium-low and simmer for 5 minutes, or until the orzo is nearly cooked.

Stir in the vegan chicken and lemon juice and simmer for another 5 minutes. Add the spinach and cook until it's just wilted.

Stir in the coconut milk. Season with salt and pepper.

Ladle the soup into bowls and enjoy.

★ ★★ THREE SALAD DRESSINGS ★★ ★
★

In summer, salads are a great way to pack in some extra veg with minimal cooking and effort, and the most important part of a salad is, of course, the dressing. Here are three banging, really quick (just look at those prep times!) ideas that you can pull together fast to get your leaves to the next level.

★ PREP 2 MINUTES ★

BALSAMIC VINAIGRETTE

MAKES 90ML (3FL OZ)

4 tablespoons extra
    virgin olive oil
1 tablespoon balsamic vinegar
2 teaspoons wholegrain mustard
salt and pepper

I love balsamic. I think my first introduction to it was at a restaurant many years ago when the bread came out before the main course with a side of oil and balsamic instead of butter. From then on I was hooked. Here's a simple vinaigrette recipe to liven up your salads.

Combine all the ingredients in a jar. Secure the lid and shake it. (If you don't have a jar, just mix them in a bowl.)

CREAMY AVOCADO DREssING

MAKES 90ML (3FL OZ)

1 avocado
1 garlic clove
10g (¼oz) dill
5 tablespoons extra
   virgin olive oil
4 tablespoons white
   wine vinegar
1–2 tablespoons lemon juice
1 teaspoon Dijon mustard
salt and pepper

Boost your salads with this creamy-cado dressing,
packed with fattiness of the good kind.

Combine all the ingredients in a food processor and blitz.
For a looser dressing, add a little more oil.

★ PREP 1 MINUTE ★

MAPLE-MUSTARD DREssING

MAKES 90ML (3FL OZ)

4 tablespoons extra
   virgin olive oil
1 tablespoon maple syrup
1 tablespoon cider vinegar
1 teaspoon Dijon mustard

A sweet, mustardy and tangy salad pick-me-up,
or a tasty dip.

Combine all the ingredients in a jar. Secure the lid and
shake it. (If you don't have a jar, just mix them in a bowl.)

CHAPTER

6

DINNER
WITH
DATES

You've had the day off and you've decided to cook your Mr or Mrs a meal to put a smile on their face. Or, you have a new date coming around and you need a recipe to impress. Look no further my beauties, the recipes in this chapter are guaranteed to get you the ride of your life.

SWYD VODKA PASTA

SERVES 2

virgin olive oil, for frying
2 large shallots, finely chopped
3 garlic cloves, thinly sliced
2 tablespoons tomato purée
2 shots vodka (I used
    SWYD vodka)
300g (10½oz) cherry
    tomatoes, chopped
2 tablespoons seasoned
    nutritional yeast (I used
    Wicked Kitchen Garlic
    & Herb Flavoured
    Nooch Seasoning)
150ml (5fl oz) plant-based
    cream (I used oat)
chilli sauce, to taste (you better
    ask your date too, you don't
    want to blow their head off)
200–250g (9oz) penne pasta
salt and pepper
chilli flakes, to garnish

It's date night and you want to cook your Tinder date a good meal before you bang each other's brains out. You must impress, but you're not very confident in the kitchen. Leave it with me – once your date has eaten this meal, they will be swinging their top off and shouting hallelujah.

Heat 1 tablespoon of oil in a large frying pan over medium heat. Add the shallots and garlic and sweat for 7 minutes, until softened. Stir in the tomato purée and cook for 3 minutes. Pour in the vodka and cook for 3 minutes, until reduced by half. Add the cherry tomatoes, seasoned nutritional yeast, plant-based cream and plenty of chilli sauce. Mix well. Season to taste with salt and pepper. Cook over medium heat for another 20 minutes.

Meanwhile, cook the penne according to packet instructions. Drain, reserving a little pasta water.

Add the cooked penne and a little of the reserved pasta water to the tomato sauce. Toss well.

Serve it up and garnish with the chilli flakes.

BUTTER BEAN BOURGUIGNON

SERVES 4–6

For the butter bean bourguignon
3 sprigs of thyme
3 sprigs of rosemary
3 sprigs of sage
30g (1oz) dried porcini
    mushrooms
250ml (9fl oz) boiling water
1 tablespoon olive oil
1 onion, diced
2 carrots, roughly chopped
60g (2¼oz) vegan lardons
5 cloves garlic, finely chopped
200g (7oz) mushrooms, trimmed
2 tablespoons tomato purée
3 × 400g (14oz) canned, drained
    and rinsed (see Note)
375ml (13fl oz) red wine
200ml (7fl oz) vegetable stock
2 tablespoons cornflour
1 tablespoon water
knob of Vegan Butter
    (see page 36)
salt and pepper
finely chopped flat-leaf
    parsley, to serve

For the potato and celeriac mash
400g (14oz) potatoes, cut
    into 2.5-cm (1-inch) cubes
300g (10½oz) celeriac, cut
    into 2.5-cm (1-inch) cubes
3 tablespoons Vegan Butter
    (see page 36)
4 teaspoons plant-based
    cream or milk
salt and pepper

I was classically trained at catering college, so bringing the classic French bourguignon to life, minus the beef, was a treat. When it comes to butter beans, the recipe is made here with canned butter beans purely for time management, but you may want to try the dried ones as well. It brings a meatier texture and consistency to the dish, plus the prep is so satisfying. As this bourguignon tastes even better the next day, prepare it a day in advance. That way, it'll be nice and ready to satisfy those post-party, comfort-food cravings.

Make the butter bean bourguignon. To make a bouquet garni, tie the sprigs of thyme, rosemary and sage together with kitchen string. (This will make it easier to pull the herbs out of the sauce before serving.)

Combine the porcini mushrooms and measured boiling water in a bowl. Set aside to rehydrate.

Heat the oil in a saucepan over medium heat. Add the onion and carrots and sweat for 7 minutes, until softened and translucent. Chuck in the vegan lardons, garlic and whole mushrooms and cook for another 7 minutes.

Drain the porcini mushrooms, reserving the porcini soaking liquid for later. (The water is full of umami flavour and will help add depth to your sauce.) Squeeze out all the excess water from the porcini, then finely chop them.

If you prefer to use dried butter beans, combine 600g (1lb 5oz) dried butter beans and enough water to cover in a large bowl and soak overnight. Drain, then add to a saucepan of water. Bring to a boil, then reduce the heat to medium-low and simmer for 1½ hours, or until tender. Drain.

Add the porcini and tomato purée to the pan and stir. Cook for 5 minutes, then add the butter beans and bouquet garni. Pour in the soaking liquid, taking care to leave out any bits of grit at the bottom. You definitely do not want that in your stock. Pour in the wine and stock.

Mix the cornflour with the measured water to make a loose paste, then add it to the sauce. Season with salt and pepper. Bring the sauce to a boil, then reduce the heat to medium-low. Simmer for 30 minutes, until sauce has thickened. Discard the bouquet garni from the bourguignon.

Meanwhile, make the potato and celeriac mash. Bring a saucepan of water to a boil. Add the potatoes and celeriac and boil for 20 minutes, until cooked through and a knife can pierce easily into the veg without resistance. Drain, then put them back into the pan.

Add the vegan butter, cream, salt and pepper and mash until silky smooth.

To serve, stir the vegan butter into the bourguignon and garnish with parsley. Serve with a generous helping of mash and you'll be on top of the world.

CREAMY ROAST GARLIC and SQUASH SOUP

SERVES 4

2 garlic bulbs
virgin olive oil, for
    brushing and frying
1 onion, thinly sliced
2 celery sticks, sliced
1 squash, peeled and dice
    into 2.5-cm (1-inch) cubes
2.5-cm (1-inch) piece of fresh
    root ginger, peeled and sliced
1 litre (35fl oz) vegetable stock
100ml (3½fl oz) plant-
    based cream
salt and white pepper
chilli flakes, to garnish
crusty bread, to serve

Glorious soup, glorious comfort. This one is an absolute beauty and I bloody love it. My favourite of prepping garlic is to roast it – once the roast garlic has cooled down, you simply grab the bulb and squeeze out this tasty, softened garlic, which can be eaten on its own or added to this soup.

Preheat the oven to 200°C (400°F), Gas Mark 6.

Slice a few millimetres off the top of the garlic bulbs so you can just see a little flesh of the garlic cloves inside their papery skins. Brush a little olive oil over the cut end and wrap them in foil. Place on a baking sheet and add the squash. Roast for 15 minutes. Remove the squash from the oven, then roast the garlic for another 15–25 minutes.

Heat 1 tablespoon of oil in a saucepan over medium heat. Add the onion and celery and sweat for 5 minutes. Add the ginger and sauté for 2 minutes, until softened. Add the squash.

Remove the garlic from the oven. When cool enough to handle, squeeze the cloves of garlic into the pan. Pour in the stock and blitz with a hand blender until smooth.

Add the plant-based cream and stir until creamy and smooth. Heat the soup over medium-high heat, until warmed through. Season with salt and pepper.

Ladle into bowls, sprinkle with chilli flakes and serve with crusty bread.

CAULIFLOWER STEAKS WITH CREAMY PURÉE and ROAST TOMATO SAUCE

SERVES 2

For the sauce
6 garlic cloves, unpeeled
3 sprigs of oregano
½ red onion, halved
250g (9oz) baby plum
    tomatoes, halved
2 tablespoons balsamic
    vinegar
salt and pepper

For the cauli steaks
1 large cauliflower
virgin olive oil, for
    brushing
salt and pepper
2 tablespoons roasted
    almonds or hazelnuts,
    crushed

For the purée
virgin olive oil, for frying
½ onion, chopped
2 garlic cloves, chopped
150g (5½oz) parsnips,
    roughly chopped
150g (5½oz) cauliflower,
    roughly chopped
3 tablespoons water
2 tablespoons plant-
    based cream
salt and pepper

Versatile cauliflower is great as a steak. Cut 'em thick and arrange 'em on silky purée, then drizzle with a tasty sauce. Perfect date-night meal.

Preheat the oven to 200°C (400°F), Gas Mark 6.

Make your sauce. Mix together all the ingredients, then spread out the mixture on a baking sheet and roast for 30 minutes, turning occasionally.

Meanwhile, make the cauli steaks. Cut the cauliflower into thick steaks, leaving the root intact. Discard any smaller leaves. Chop the ends off the cauliflower and reserve for the purée. Brush oil over the steaks and large leaves. Season with salt and pepper.

Transfer only the steaks to a baking sheet, leaving the large leaves to the side. Roast the steaks for 10 minutes. Add the cauliflower leaves to the sheet. Turn the steaks and bake for another 10 minutes.

Now, make the purée. Heat 2 tablespoons of olive oil in a frying pan over medium-high heat. Add the onion and garlic and sweat for 3–4 minutes, until softened. Add the parsnips, chopped cauliflower and any reserved ends from the cauli steaks. Add the measured water and cover. Reduce the heat to low and cook for 5–10 minutes, until tender. Drain and combine it with the cream in a food processor. Season with salt and pepper and purée until smooth. Season to taste. Transfer the purée to a saucepan and keep warm. Clean the bowl of the food processor.

Remove the roasted tomatoes from the oven. Discard the oregano sprigs. Squeeze the roasted garlic cloves into the cleaned food processor. Add the tomatoes, onion and any juices. Blitz until smooth. If it appears too thick, thin it out with a splash of water.

Place the purée on plates. Top with the cauliflower steaks and leaves, drizzle over the tomato sauce and garnish with the nuts.

CREAMY TOMATO RISOTTO

SERVES 2

6 good-quality tomatoes
20g (¾oz) basil, plus 10g
  (¼oz) to garnish
3 tablespoons extra virgin
  olive oil
1 onion, finely chopped
2 garlic cloves, finely chopped
200g (7oz) risotto rice
2 tablespoons tomato purée
100ml (3½fl oz) white wine
80g (2¾oz) cherry tomatoes,
  halved or quartered
750ml (26fl oz) vegetable stock
100ml (3½fl oz) oat milk or
  single soy cream (optional)
knob of Vegan Butter
  (see page 36, optional)
vegan Parmesan cheese
  (optional)
salt and pepper

Your tomatoes are essential to the risotto's flavour. Bypass the bland, watery tomatoes on special and splurge on some juicy, flavourful tomatoes that will bring this dish to life.

Put the tomatoes and basil in a food processor. Add some salt and pepper and blitz until smooth. Line a bowl with muslin, then pour in the tomato mixture and squeeze out the tomato-basil water. I managed to get 250ml (9fl oz).

Heat 2 tablespoons of oil in a large frying pan over medium heat. Add the onion and sweat for 7 minutes, until translucent. Add the garlic and sweat for another 2 minutes. Stir in the rice and mix for 3 minutes. Add the tomato purée and cook for 3 minutes. Add the wine and cook for 3–5 minutes, until the wine has been absorbed.

Stir in the cherry tomatoes. Gradually pour in the tomato-basil water and mix until it's completely absorbed. Add a ladle of the vegetable stock and stir every 30 seconds until absorbed. Repeat with more stock, a ladle at a time, until the rice is cooked.

If you like, add the oat milk to make it creamier and finish with a knob of vegan butter and vegan Parmesan.

Garnish with basil leaves and serve.

⋆ ⋆⋆ VEGAN BUTTER ⋆⋆ ⋆ AUBERGINE CURRY

SERVES 2

For the aubergines

2.5-cm (1-inch) fresh root
   ginger, finely chopped
2 garlic cloves, crushed
4 tablespoons unsweetened
   soy or coconut yogurt
1 tablespoon garam masala
1 teaspoon each of ground
   cumin, chilli powder
   and ground coriander
600g (1lb 5oz) baby
   aubergines, halved
salt and pepper

For the curry

3 tablespoons coconut
   oil or Vegan Butter
   (see page 36)
1 onion, chopped
4 garlic cloves,
   finely chopped
2.5-cm (1-inch) fresh root
   ginger, finely chopped
1 teaspoon ground coriander
chilli powder, to taste
2 tablespoons tomato purée
400g (14oz) can
   chopped tomatoes
250ml (9fl oz) plant-based
   cream (I used oat)
15g (½oz) coriander,
   chopped, to garnish
salt and pepper
golden vegetable rice,
   to serve

For the salad

½ cucumber, thinly sliced
¼ red onion, thinly sliced

Curry, curry, curry. Oy! Oy! Oy! Another day, another curry. I took inspiration from the famed butter chicken but replaced the chicken with aubergines, which have a similar meaty texture and can absorb flavour well. Just be sure to leave it in the marinade overnight.

Make the aubergines. In a large bowl, combine all the ingredients, except for the aubergines. Mix well. Add the aubergines and mix to evenly coat. Cover the bowl with clingfilm and refrigerate for at least 3 hours but preferably overnight (to maximize the flavours in the aubergines).

Preheat the oven to 190°C (375°F), Gas Mark 5.

Transfer the marinated aubergines to a baking dish and bake for 20–25 minutes, until tender.

Meanwhile, make the curry. Melt the coconut oil (or vegan butter) in a saucepan over medium heat. Add the onion and sweat for 7 minutes, or until translucent. Add the garlic and ginger and cook for another 3 minutes. Add the ground coriander and chilli powder.

Stir in the tomato purée and cook for 1 minute. Add the canned tomatoes and plant-based cream and simmer for 10 minutes, stirring occasionally.

Add the aubergines. The spicy aubergine coating will also flavour the sauce. If you find it too dry, add a splash of water. Reduce the heat to medium-low and simmer for 10 minutes.

Prepare the rice according to packet instructions. Combine the salad ingredients, season with salt and pepper and mix well.

To serve, transfer the curry into a serving bowl. Sprinkle with coriander. Serve with rice and salad.

CREAMY VEG BAKE

SERVES 4

Vegan Butter (see page 36),
    for greasing
2 potatoes, thinly sliced
2 parsnips, thinly sliced
2 carrots, thinly sliced
2 onions, thinly sliced
½ small celeriac, thinly sliced
5 garlic cloves, crushed
a generous grating of nutmeg
500ml (18fl oz) plant-based
    cream (I used oat)
grated vegan cheese
salt and pepper

Want a tasty side dish with your Sunday dinner? This delicious and hearty vegan bake works wonders, combining creamy layers of potato and caramelized onions with melted cheese. The veg should be thinly sliced, about approximately 3mm (⅛ inch) thick. You can use a knife to do this, or if you're feeling brave, a mandoline. Be careful using a mandoline as they are super dangerous – please take your time as one slip could cause a serious injury.

Preheat the oven to 190°C (375°F), Gas Mark 5. Grease a 2-litre (3½-pint) casserole.

In a large bowl, combine the sliced vegetables, garlic and nutmeg. Season well with salt and pepper. Pour in half the plant-based cream and mix with your hands.

Transfer the mixture to the prepared dish. (Don't worry about being too neat – just avoid having any large gaps.) Pour over any cream from the bowl, then drizzle over with the remaining half. Press the veg down. Cover tightly with foil and bake for 30 minutes.

It'll be steaming hot! Carefully uncover, then sprinkle with grated cheese. Cover again and bake for 20–25 minutes, until the cheese is golden brown and the veg are tender.

LASAGNE

· SERVES 4 ·

For the tomato sauce
virgin olive oil, for frying
1 red onion, finely chopped
4 garlic cloves, finely chopped
1 courgette, chopped
1 pepper, any colour, cored,
    deseeded and chopped
1 tablespoon tomato purée
175ml (6fl oz) red wine
500g (1lb 2oz) plant mince
800g (1lb 12oz) passata
few sprigs of rosemary
    or basil, finely chopped
salt and pepper

For the tofu sauce
600g (1lb 5oz) silken tofu
2 tablespoons nutritional yeast
½ tablespoon cornflour
1 teaspoon garlic powder
1 teaspoon wholegrain mustard
1 teaspoon cider vinegar
200ml (7fl oz) plant-based
    milk, plus extra to thin out
salt and pepper

For the lasagne
300g (10½oz) lasagne sheets
squirt of ketchup
200g (7oz) grated
    vegan Parmesan

For the basil oil (optional)
3 sprigs of basil
2 tablespoons extra
    virgin olive oil
pinch of salt

A baked dish full of little Italian kisses. I was never much of a lasagne fan, but I've recently come to enjoy its comforting properties. Plus, it's really good to serve when you want to prepare something delicious but easy.

Make the tomato sauce. Preheat the oven to 190°C (375°F), Gas Mark 5.

Heat 1 tablespoon of oil in a large frying pan over medium heat. Add the onion and sweat for 7 minutes, until translucent. Add the garlic, courgette and pepper and sweat for 5 minutes, or until softened. Stir in the tomato purée and cook for another 2 minutes. Add the wine, scraping up the stuck bits on your pan with a wooden spoon. Cook for another 5 minutes, or until reduced by half.

Add the plant mince and cook for 3 minutes. Stir in the passata and rosemary (or basil). Bring to a boil, then simmer for 10 minutes. Season with salt and pepper. Your sauce is ready to use.

Meanwhile, make the tofu sauce. Put all the ingredients into a blender and blitz until creamy. If needed, add more plant-based milk to get the right consistency.

Time to assemble the lasagne. In an ovenproof dish, spread the tomato filling on the bottom. Next, add a layer of lasagne sheets, tomato sauce, tofu cream and a sprinkle of the vegan cheese. Repeat the layers until you've run out of sauce. Finish with a layer of vegan cheese. Bake for 35–40 minutes, until nicely browned on top.

Make the basil oil, if using. With a pestle and mortar, combine all the ingredients and smash until smooth. Drizzle the basil oil over the lasagne and serve.

PATATAS BRAVAS
SERVES 4

6 good-sized potatoes, cut
    into 2-cm (¾-inch) cubes
1 red pepper
virgin olive oil, for frying
2 shallots, finely chopped
5 garlic cloves, finely chopped
1 tablespoon tomato purée
1½ tablespoons smoked paprika
1 teaspoon cayenne pepper
400g (14oz) can chopped
    tomatoes
2 tablespoons cider vinegar
dash of maple syrup
salt and pepper

My first introduction to Patatas Bravas was in my Ibiza days. I was too busy raving to enjoy a substantial meal so when I discovered them it was a game changer. Now, I order it every time I go to Spain. Simple but delicious.

Preheat the oven to 200°C (400°F), Gas Mark 6.

Place the potatoes in a bowl of salted water and soak for 1 hour.

Place the pepper into the oven and roast for 30 minutes. Set aside to cool.

Heat 100ml (3½fl oz) oil in a deep frying pan over high heat. Drain the potatoes and pat dry. (Be sure the potatoes are completely dry before adding them to the oil; otherwise, they will spit in the oil and you may burn yourself.) Carefully add the potatoes to the oil and fry for 20 minutes, turning them frequently, so they cook evenly all over. Using a slotted spoon, transfer the potatoes to a plate lined with kitchen paper to drain. Keep warm.

Heat 1 tablespoon of oil in a frying pan over medium-high heat. Add the shallots and garlic and sweat for 5 minutes, until translucent. Add the tomato purée and cook for another 3 minutes. Stir in the paprika and cayenne pepper. Add the roasted pepper, chopped tomatoes, cider vinegar and maple syrup and simmer for 3 minutes. Transfer the mixture to a blender, season with salt and pepper and blend until smooth. Set aside.

Put them on a plate and serve with the bravas sauce.

THREE PICKLES *and* RELISHES

I always think homemade pickles are well impressive, they jazz up any salads, noodles or wraps and are a great way to add lots of dishes to the table with minimal input on the day. Here are three of my favourites.

PREP 5 MINUTES ★ COOK 50 MINUTES

RED ONION RELISH

SERVES 6–8

virgin olive oil, for frying
3 red onions, halved and
    thinly sliced
1 garlic clove, grated
4 tablespoons sugar
large pinch of salt
6 tablespoons balsamic vinegar

Sticky sweet-and sour-onions make a tasty condiment for vegan burgers.

Heat 2 tablespoons of oil in a frying pan over medium-low heat. Add the onions and garlic and cook low and slow for 30 minutes, until the onions are translucent and softened.

Add the sugar, salt and balsamic. Cook for another 20 minutes, allowing the flavours to meld.

Transfer the mixture to a sterilized glass jar (run it through a very hot wash in the dishwasher). Store in the fridge and consume within 4 days.

Recipe pictured overleaf

SWEETCORN RELISH

SERVES 6–8

virgin olive oil, for frying
2 shallots, finely chopped
4 sweetcorn cobs, kernels
    shaven off
½ teaspoon salt
175ml (6fl oz) cider vinegar
60g (2¼oz) caster sugar

*We used to buy store-bought sweetcorn relish that came
in squeezy bottles. I would load it on burgers. These days,
I'm opting for something healthier. This homemade version
tastes even better than the one I had as a kid. A little bite
to the corn makes all the difference.*

Heat 1 tablespoon of oil in a medium saucepan over
medium-high heat. Add the shallots and sweat for
3–5 minutes, until softened. Add the corn and salt
and cook for 3 minutes.

Stir in the cider vinegar and sugar. Bring to a boil,
then reduce the heat to medium-low and simmer for
15 minutes. Transfer the mixture to a sterilized glass jar
(run it through a very hot wash in the dishwasher) and set
aside to cool. It will keep in the sealed jar in the fridge for up
to 4 days.

Serve this tasty condiment over salads, vegan hot dogs,
sandwiches and plant burgers.

Recipe pictured overleaf

PICKLED VEGETABLES

MAKES 1 MASON JAR 1.5L (2¾ PINT)

500ml (18fl oz) white
    wine vinegar
500ml (18fl oz) water
3 tablespoons sugar
2 tablespoons sea salt
1 tablespoon black peppercorns
1 tablespoon coriander seeds
1 garlic bulb, cloves
    separated and peeled
1 red onion, root end intact
    and quartered
½ cauliflower, cut into
    florets (see Note)
150g (5½oz) radishes,
    halved if large
3 red chillies, quartered
4 sprigs of rosemary

NOTE
Discarded cauliflower leaves
can be kept in the fridge
and cooked like cabbage.

Readers are often instructed to remove chilli seeds, but I never understood why. Apparently its where all the 'heat' is in the chilli, but that's why we're using them! FFS – just keep 'em in! That's essential here.

In a medium saucepan, combine the vinegar, measured water, sugar and salt. Boil until the sugar has dissolved. Set aside to cool.

To a clean, sterilized 1.5-litre (2¾-pint) Mason jar, add the peppercorns and coriander seeds. Add in the vegetables, stuffing the chillies and rosemary down the sides.

Pour in the pickling liquid until it's about 2mm (1/16 inch) from the top. Close the jar, then set aside to cool. Refrigerate until needed.

Leftover pickles should be consumed within 3 weeks.

CHAPTER

7

TOOTH-
KILLERS

FEELING NUTTY AND FRUITY BARS 170

AVOCADO CHOCOLATE MOUSSE 172

SALTED CARAMEL STICKY PUDDING 174

CRÈME BRÛLÉE 176

PEAR FRANGIPANE TART 178

WAFFLING WAFFLES 179

THREE SORBETS
MANGO SORBET 180
BLUEBERRY SORBET 182
STRAWBERRY SORBET 183

I just loved the pastry section in my culinary college years and sampling the goods as I cooked. I used to have an incredibly sweet tooth and, while it has chilled out over the years, I still love a good pud. Here are some very quick, simple puds, as well as a few that take a little time and skill. Toothbrushes at the ready, we're going IN WITH OUR SPOONS...

FEELING NUTTY and FRUITY BARS

MAKES 20 BARS

150g (5½oz) unsalted peanuts
150g (5½oz) shelled
  pistachios nuts
150g (5½oz) cashew nuts
150g (5½oz) almonds
300g (10½oz) peanut butter
200g (7oz) dried
  apricots, chopped
200g (7oz) dates,
  stoned and chopped
200g (7oz) raisins, chopped
100g (3½oz) chia seeds
100ml (3½fl oz) maple syrup
60g (2¼oz) vegan chocolate
  chips (optional)
sprinkle of sea salt
virgin olive oil, for greasing

These bars are perfect when you're training. For long bike rides, I'll wrap them up, put them in my back pocket and eat them when I need an energy fix. They also make a reliable snack with a cup of tea. I love nuts, dried fruit and peanut butter, so I've combined them in this one recipe. Absolutely BANGING.

Put all the nuts into a frying pan. Dry-fry over medium heat, tossing occasionally, until they're slightly roasted and the oils are released.

In a blender or food processor, combine all the ingredients and pulse until well combined.

Grease a rimmed baking sheet, then add the mixture and flatten out. Place the sheet into the fridge for 30 minutes to firm up, then cut your bars to size. These will keep in a sealed container for a week.

AVOCADO CHOCOLATE MOUSSE

SERVES 2

100g (3½oz) dark vegan
  chocolate (70% cocoa)
3 tablespoons cocoa powder
3 tablespoons maple syrup
4 tablespoons plant-based
  cream (I used oat)
½ vanilla pod or 1 teaspoon
  vanilla extract
2 ripe avocados
pinch of salt
4 tablespoons plant-based
  milk, plus extra to thin out
crushed pistachio nuts,
  to decorate

Avocado and chocolate??? Trust me, they work unbelievably well together. Top with crunchy pistachios or fresh fruit (or both) and prepare yourself for a delicious treat. You'll want to use the seeds from a vanilla pod, but vanilla extract is an acceptable substitute. Just be sure to stay away from the essence, which gives an artificial taste.

In a microwaveable bowl, combine the vegan chocolate, cocoa, maple syrup and plant-based cream. Nuke in the microwave on medium-low heat, checking and stirring at 30-second intervals, until the chocolate has melted.

Scrape out the seeds from the vanilla pod with the back of a knife. In a food processor, combine all the ingredients and blend until smooth. Occasionally, push down any mixture stuck on the sides. The mixture should be light and airy. If needed, add a little more plant-based milk to loosen to your desired consistency.

Transfer the mousse into nice glasses. Sprinkle with pistachios and serve.

SALTED CARAMEL STICKY PUDDING

SERVES 6

For the sticky pudding
100g (3½oz) Vegan Butter (see page 36), plus extra for greasing
200g (7oz) pitted dates
100ml (3½fl oz) water
100g (3½oz) light soft brown sugar
200g (7oz) self-raising flour, sifted
1 teaspoon bicarbonate of soda
225ml (8floz) soy milk
40g (1½oz) chopped pecans, plus extra to serve
1 tablespoon white wine vinegar
plant-based cream or vanilla vegan ice cream, to serve

For the salted caramel sauce
100g (3½oz) Vegan Butter (see page 36)
80g (2¾oz) light soft brown sugar
2 tablespoons maple syrup
125ml (4fl oz) canned coconut milk
pinch of sea salt

Chuck your diet plans outta the window – you're gonna need a post-dessert run, bike ride or cardio sesh to burn off all them calories! Sure, this dessert is far from healthy, but that's the point. Once in a while, I give myself the freedom to indulge and this pudding hits the spot. It's spongy and sticky sweet. You'll need your BIG spoon for this one.

Make the sticky pudding. Preheat the oven to 190°C (375°F), Gas Mark 5. Grease a 1.2-litre (2-pint) baking dish with vegan butter.

Combine the dates and the measured water in a small saucepan and bring to a simmer. Simmer for 3 minutes, until the dates are softened. Using a fork, mash the dates into the water until gooey.

Using an electric mixer, cream the vegan butter and sugar in a bowl, until light and fluffy. (If you don't have a whisk, some elbow grease will do – just mix with a hand whisk.) Add the flour and bicarbonate of soda and mix until dry and crumbly.

Gradually pour in the milk and mix until smooth. Add the mashed dates, pecans and vinegar and fold it until bubbles begin to form. (This is the vinegar reacting with the bicarbonate of soda.) Pour the batter into the prepared dish. Bake for 50 minutes, until a skewer inserted into the centre comes out clean. It's ready to rock.

Meanwhile, make the salted caramel sauce. Combine all the ingredients in a saucepan over medium heat. Do NOT let it boil. Reduce the heat to medium-low and gently simmer for 10 minutes, stirring occasionally. Set aside. The sauce will thicken slightly.

Pierce a few holes over the pud. Drizzle with enough sauce for it to sit on top and seep into the holes. Pour the remaining sauce into a small jug or bowl to serve alongside the dessert.

Serve with plant-based cream or a nice dollop of ice cream. Savour every flavour... or demolish it within seconds like I did. Y-U-M.

GUEST CHEF: THIBAULT COURTOISIER
CRÈME BRÛLÉE
· SERVES 2 ·

375ml (13fl oz) plant-
  based cream
150–200g (5½–7oz)
  caster sugar
33g (1oz) cashew nuts
15g (½oz) cornflour
1 vanilla pod or 1 teaspoon
  vanilla extract

For the topping
1½–2 tablespoons
  caster sugar
fresh fruit, to decorate
  (optional)

If you're an avid viewer of Bake Off: The Professionals, *you may recognize Thibault Courtoisier as the show's 2020 winner. Since I rarely watch television, I only first heard of him from my mate, Tim Corrigan who owns the Milk & Sugar coffee shops across Cardiff. One day, he came over with vegan macarons prepared by Thibault that were seriously OFF-THE-SCALE tasty. I messaged Thibault on social media and the next thing I know, he's showing me how to make these delicious macarons in his kitchen (check them out on my Youtube channel). I recently bumped into him in the supermarket, so asked if he'd like to contribute a guest dessert in the book, and here it is. This serves two, but the first time I sampled these crème brûlée, I nearly ate them both. They're THAT good.*

In a saucepan, combine the plant-based cream, sugar, cashew nuts and cornflour. With the back of a knife, scrape out the seeds from the vanilla pod and add them to the pan.

Using a hand mixer, blend until the cashews are coarsely ground. Bring to a boil, stirring constantly with a whisk.

Pour the mixture into a food processor. Using the smoothie attachment, blitz until smooth. Using a sieve, strain the mixture into 2 ramekins. Chill in the fridge for 4–6 hours.

To serve, sprinkle the crème brûlées with the caster sugar. Using a kitchen blowtorch, caramelize the sugar on top. (Alternatively, pop them under a hot grill for about 1 minute. Keep an eye on them – they can burn quickly.)

Decorate with fruit, if you wish, then get set to devour them.

PEAR FRANGIPANE TART

SERVES 4-6

plain flour, for dusting
500g (1lb 2oz) pack of vegan
   ready-made shortcrust pastry
140g (5oz) ground almonds
70g (2½oz) oat flour
1 teaspoon baking powder
1 teaspoon cornflour
100g (3½oz) Vegan Butter
   (see page 36)
100g (3½oz) caster sugar
1 teaspoon vanilla extract
5 tablespoons almond milk
blueberry jam
2 ripe pears, peeled, cored,
   quartered and thinly sliced
handful of chopped almonds,
   for sprinkling
coconut sugar, for sprinkling

Frangipane is a fun tart to make but it's even more fun to eat – try tucking into it with some delicious vegan vanilla ice cream or Strawberry Sorbet (see page 183).

Preheat the oven to 180°C (350°F), Gas Mark 4.

Roll out the pastry on a lightly floured surface, about 5cm (2 inches) wider than the circumference of your flan tin. (I used a 22-cm/8½-inch fluted flan tin.) Carefully pick up your pastry so it doesn't break and line your tin with it. Trim off any excess pastry. Using a fork, prick the pastry base all over. To blind bake the pastry base, line it with baking paper and fill with baking beans (or dried beans). Blind bake for 15 minutes, then remove the paper and beans.

Meanwhile, prepare the frangipane filling. In a large bowl, combine the ground almonds, oat flour, baking powder and cornflour.

Using an electric mixer, cream the vegan butter, sugar and vanilla extract in a bowl, until light and fluffy. (If you don't have a whisk, some elbow grease will do – just mix with a hand whisk.) Stir in the almond mixture. Pour in the almond milk to create a paste.

Using a pastry brush, spread a thin layer of blueberry jam onto the pastry base. (If you'd like a thicker layer, go for gold.) Add the frangipane, spreading it out evenly with a spatula.

Fan the pears over the tart. (We want it to look all fancy and posh!) Sprinkle with chopped almonds and coconut sugar. Bake for 45 minutes, until golden.

Set aside to cool, then serve.

WAFFLING WAFFLES

SERVES 2–4

For the waffles
140g (5oz) self-raising
    flour, sifted
3 tablespoons icing sugar
2 teaspoon baking powder
pinch of salt
300ml (10fl oz) almond milk
2 teaspoons vegetable
    or sunflower oil
2 teaspoons vanilla extract

**For the peanut butter
    and maple sauce**
5 tablespoons maple syrup
2 tablespoons peanut butter
1 teaspoon vanilla extract
    or paste

For the chocolate sauce
200ml (7fl oz) plant-
    based cream
200g (7oz) vegan dark
    chocolate, finely chopped

For the toppings
1 banana, sliced
vegan marshmallows
fruit (kiwi, raspberries,
    blueberries, strawberries
    or blackberries)
High-Protein Granola
    (see page 113)
vegan ice cream,
    cream or yogurt

*There are so many ways to enjoy them, but I love tucking
into a sweet waffle. Here are some topping ideas but feel
free to make up your own. At the risk of sounding obvious,
you will need a waffle maker for this recipe.*

Make the waffles. Preheat the waffle maker until hot.

In a bowl, combine the flour, icing sugar, baking powder
and salt.

In another bowl, combine the almond milk, oil and vanilla.
Add the wet ingredients to the dry and mix well to make
the batter.

Pour some batter into the waffle maker and cook for
5 minutes. Transfer to a plate, then repeat until all the
batter is used.

Make the peanut butter and maple sauce. In a small
bowl, combine the maple syrup, peanut butter and vanilla.
Mix well.

Make the chocolate sauce. Bring a saucepan of water to
a boil. Place a heatproof glass bowl over the pan, making
sure the bottom doesn't touch the water. Pour the plant-
based cream into the bowl and heat up. Add the vegan
chocolate and stir until silky smooth.

To serve, drizzle the sweet peanuty goodness over
your waffles, top with banana and tuck in. Or drizzle
the chocolate sauce over the waffles and top with
marshmallows. Or serve with your favourite toppings.
No matter what, prepare to get messy.

THREE SORBETS

★

In the 16th century, noble families would serve sorbet to cleanse the palate. And when I trained at my college's on-site restaurant, we often served sorbet after the fish course. These days, we enjoy sorbet for completely different reasons. It's a refreshing treat on a hot summer's day, or it's a good option when you're out and it's gelato o'clock for your non-vegan pals.

★ PREP 10 MINUTES, PLUS FREEZING ★

MANGO SORBET

SERVES 2

3 mangoes, chopped
4 tablespoons maple syrup
1 tablespoon lime juice, plus
    extra to serve (optional)
black sesame seeds,
    to serve (optional)

The original summer cooler. Just perfect.

Put the mango in a freezer bag and freeze for 3–4 hours, until frozen.

In a high-powered blender, combine the mango, maple syrup and lime juice and blitz until it has a sorbet consistency. If the consistency isn't right, transfer the mixture to a bowl and freeze for 2–3 hours, until firm.

The sorbet can be stored in the freezer for up to 2 weeks. When ready to serve, transfer the sorbet to the fridge and chill for 15 minutes, until slightly softened.

Serve with black sesame seeds and lime juice, if you wish.

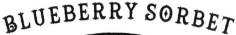

200g (7oz) frozen blueberries
50g (1¾oz) caster sugar
2 tablespoons lemon juice
2 tablespoons vodka, gin or
    rum (optional, see Note)

NOTE
If you want to freeze the sorbet,
add a little alcohol to keep the
texture softer once frozen.

*This sorbet has a pleasant sourness, followed by a sweet
tang – and it's incredibly refreshing on the palate. Geez,
I sound like silver service waiter at a posh restaurant. (Ha!)*

Set the blueberries aside for 10 minutes.

Combine all the ingredients in a high-powered blender
and whizz until smooth. (If it's too hard to blend, leave
for a few minutes and try again.)

Serve immediately as a soft-scoop sorbet. (Alternatively,
spoon the sorbet into a small container and freeze for at
least 1 hour until firm. Place in the fridge for 15 minutes
before serving.)

STRAWBERRY SORBET

SERVES 2

200g (7oz) frozen strawberries
50g (1¾oz) caster sugar
2 tablespoons lemon juice
2 tablespoons vodka, gin or rum
**   (optional, see Note)**

NOTE
If you want to freeze the sorbet,
add a little alcohol to keep the
texture softer once frozen.

The taste of this sorbet relies on sweet, quality strawberries.
It's fantastic on its own or with the Pear Frangipane Tart
(see page 178).

Set the strawberries aside for 10 minutes.

Combine all the ingredients in a high-powered blender
and whizz until smooth. (If it's too hard to blend, leave
for a few minutes and try again.)

Serve immediately as a soft-scoop sorbet. (Alternatively,
spoon the sorbet into a small container and freeze for at
least 1 hour until firm. Place in the fridge for 15 minutes
before serving.)

INDEX

GLOSSARY

UK	US
Aubergine	Eggplant
Baking paper	Parchment paper
Beans, butter	Beans, lima
Broccoli, Tenderstem	Broccoli, baby (broccolini)
Cabbage, white	Cabbage, green
Celeriac	Celery root
Chilli flakes	Dried red pepper flakes
Chinese leaf lettuce	Napa cabbage
Cider vinegar	Apple cider vinegar
Clingfilm	Plastic wrap
Coriander	If referring to the leaves, cilantro
Cornflour	Cornstarch
Courgette	Zucchini
Fast-action dried yeast	Active dry yeast
Flan tin	Tart pan
Flour, plain	Flour, all-purpose
Flour, self-raising	Use all-purpose flour plus 1 tsp. baking powder per 125 g of flour
Flour, strong white	Flour, white bread
Giant couscous	Israeli (pearl) couscous
Jug	Liquid measuring cup or pitcher
Kitchen paper	Paper towels
Lardons, vegan	Bacon pieces, vegan
Lasagne sheets	Lasagna noodles
Lolly	Ice pops
Mangetout	Snow peas
Mushrooms, chestnut	Mushrooms, cremini
Muslin	Cheesecloth
Petit pois	Young peas
Passata	Tomato puree or sauce
Pastry base	Pastry shell
Plant mince	Meatless plant crumbles
Porridge oats	Rolled oats
Potatoes, floury (King Edward and Maris Piper)	Potatoes, starchy (russets and Yukon Gold)
Potatoes, waxy	Potatoes, new
Rapeseed oil	Canola oil
Rocket	Arugula
Spring onion	Scallion
Sugar, caster	Sugar, superfine
Sugar, icing	Sugar, confectioners'
Swede	Rutabaga
Sweetcorn	Corn
Tea towel	Dish towel
Tomato purée	Tomato paste
Vanilla pod	Vanilla bean

COOK'S NOTES

Standard level spoon measurements are used in all recipes.
1 tablespoon = one 15ml spoon
1 teaspoon = one 5ml spoon

Fresh herbs should be used unless otherwise stated. If unavailable,
use dried herbs as an alternative but halve the quantities stated.

Ovens should be preheated to the specific temperature – if using
a fan-assisted oven, follow manufacturer's instructions for adjusting
the time and the temperature.

All microwave information is based on a 650-watt oven.
Follow manufacturer's instructions for an oven with a different wattage.

Pepper should be freshly ground black pepper unless otherwise stated.

This book includes dishes made with nuts and nut derivatives.
It is advisable for those with known allergic reactions to nuts and
nut derivatives and those who may be potentially vulnerable to these
allergies, such as pregnant and nursing mothers, invalids, the elderly,
babies and children, to avoid dishes made with nuts and nut oils.
It is also prudent to check the labels of pre-prepared ingredients
for the possible inclusion of nut derivatives.

Vegans should look for the 'V' symbol on a cheese to ensure
it is made with vegan rennet.

ACKNOWLEDGEMENTS

This book is to all of you that are trying to kick things like addiction, mental health, anxiety, or anything that you're finding hard. It isn't easy, but remember there's always light at the end of the tunnel. Keep going, you're all amazing and don't let anyone tell you any different. And to those who feel that they don't fit in, embrace your weirdness as that's what makes you YOU!

I would also like to take this opportunity to give a huge thank you to the teams at Octopus and Smith & Gilmour for giving me the opportunity to write my third book and all the hard work they've put into making this book. I'd like to thank John, Nik and Dave at John Noel management for the work that they do for me. Thanks to the two Kings, John and Dylan, and the two Simons, as well as to the team at SWYD tattoo and Barbers. And finally to my therapist Chip Somers, who over the last eight months has done so much to help me slowly get back on my feet again and help me through my sobriety. Thank you mate.

Here's to anyone that has helped me along the way: if your name's not down you know who you are, thank you. And to those that pulled my pants down, thanks for the lessons.